TRIBES OF THE
SOUTHERN WOODLANDS

✛

TIME®
LIFE
BOOKS

Other Publications:

WEIGHT WATCHERS® SMART CHOICE RECIPE COLLECTION
TRUE CRIME
THE ART OF WOODWORKING
LOST CIVILIZATIONS
ECHOES OF GLORY
THE NEW FACE OF WAR
HOW THINGS WORK
WINGS OF WAR
CREATIVE EVERYDAY COOKING
COLLECTOR'S LIBRARY OF THE UNKNOWN
CLASSICS OF WORLD WAR II
TIME-LIFE LIBRARY OF CURIOUS AND UNUSUAL FACTS
AMERICAN COUNTRY
VOYAGE THROUGH THE UNIVERSE
THE THIRD REICH
THE TIME-LIFE GARDENER'S GUIDE
MYSTERIES OF THE UNKNOWN
TIME FRAME
FIX IT YOURSELF
FITNESS, HEALTH & NUTRITION
SUCCESSFUL PARENTING
HEALTHY HOME COOKING
UNDERSTANDING COMPUTERS
LIBRARY OF NATIONS
THE ENCHANTED WORLD
THE KODAK LIBRARY OF CREATIVE PHOTOGRAPHY
GREAT MEALS IN MINUTES
THE CIVIL WAR
PLANET EARTH
COLLECTOR'S LIBRARY OF THE CIVIL WAR
THE EPIC OF FLIGHT
THE GOOD COOK
WORLD WAR II
HOME REPAIR AND IMPROVEMENT
THE OLD WEST

For information on and a full description of any of the
Time-Life Books series listed above, please call
1-800-621-7026 or write:
Reader Information
Time-Life Customer Service
P.O. Box C-32068
Richmond, Virginia 23261-2068

This volume is one of a series that chronicles the history and culture of the Native Americans. Other books in the series include:

THE FIRST AMERICANS
THE SPIRIT WORLD
THE EUROPEAN CHALLENGE
PEOPLE OF THE DESERT
THE WAY OF THE WARRIOR
THE BUFFALO HUNTERS
REALM OF THE IROQUOIS
THE MIGHTY CHIEFTAINS
KEEPERS OF THE TOTEM
CYCLES OF LIFE
WAR FOR THE PLAINS

The Cover: Wearing a coyote-skin headdress and dazzling face paint, an Oklahoma Cherokee celebrates his cultural heritage during a modern powwow commemorating the 1838 forced migration known as the Trail of Tears. More than 10,000 men, women, and children of five tribes—Cherokee, Creek, Choctaw, Chickasaw, and Seminole—died during the ordeal of their removal from the Southeast to the government-designated reserves in the Indian Territory, present-day Oklahoma.

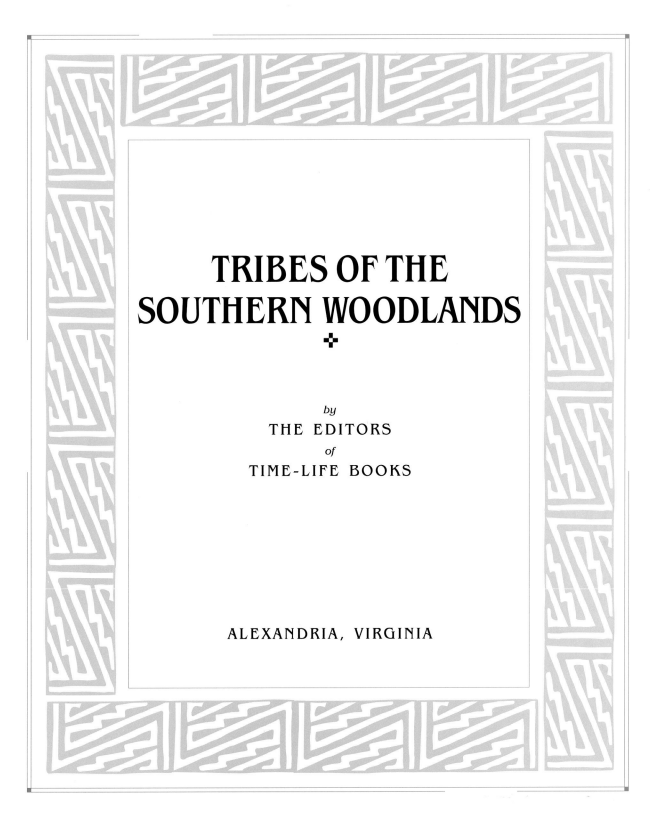

TRIBES OF THE SOUTHERN WOODLANDS

✣

by
THE EDITORS
of
TIME-LIFE BOOKS

ALEXANDRIA, VIRGINIA

THE AMERICAN INDIANS

SERIES EDITOR: Henry Woodhead
Administrative Editor: Jane Edwin

Editorial Staff for *Tribes of the Southern Woodlands*
Senior Art Director: Ray Ripper
Picture Editor: Susan V. Kelly
Text Editors: John Newton (principal), Stephen G.
Hyslop
Writer: Stephanie Lewis
Associate Editors/Research: Kirk E. Denkler, Robert
H. Wooldridge, Jr. (principals), Trudy W. Pearson
Assistant Art Director: Susan M. Gibas
Senior Copyeditor: Ann Lee Bruen
Picture Coordinator: David Beard
Editorial Assistant: Gemma Villanueva

Special Contributors: Amy Aldrich, Ronald H. Bailey,
Marfé Ferguson Delano, Thomas Lewis, Susan Per-
ry, David S. Thomson (text); Martha Lee Becking-
ton, R. Curtis Kopf, Elizabeth Pope, Marilyn Mur-
phy Terrell (research); Barbara L. Klein (index).

Correspondents: Elisabeth Kraemer-Singh (Bonn),
Christine Hinze (London), Christina Lieberman
(New York), Maria Vincenza Aloisi (Paris), Ann
Natanson (Rome). Valuable assistance was also
provided by: Barbara Gevene Hertz (Copenhagen),
Daniel Donnelly (New York).

General Consultants
Raymond D. Fogelson is Professor of Anthropology at the University of Chicago, whose research
and teaching interests include American Indian
ethnohistory and ethnology, religion, and psycho-
logical anthropology. He has written many articles
focusing on the southeastern Indians, the history
of anthropology, and conception of self and per-
sonhood in different societies. Dr. Fogelson is also
the editor of several books, including *The Anthropology of Power*. He is a fellow of the American Anthropological Association and past president of
the American Society for Ethnohistory.

Michael D. Green is Professor of History at the University of Kentucky where he teaches courses in
the history of Native Americans and of United
States Indian policy. A specialist in southeastern
Indians, Dr. Green focuses his research on the political and social history of the Creeks. He is the
author *The Politics of Indian Removal: Creek Government and Society in Crisis, The Creeks*, and several other books. Dr. Green has been a fellow of
the Newberry Library's D'Arcy McNickle Center for
the History of the American Indian.

Frederick E. Hoxie is director of the D'Arcy Mc-
Nickle Center for the History of the American Indi-
an at the Newberry Library in Chicago. Dr. Hoxie is
the author of *A Final Promise: The Campaign to As-
similate the Indians 1880-1920* and other works.
He has served as a history consultant to the
Cheyenne River and Standing Rock Sioux tribes,
Little Big Horn College archives, and the Senate
Select Committee on Indian Affairs. He is a trustee
of the National Museum of the American Indian in
Washington, D.C.

Special Consultant
Duane King is the assistant director of the Smith-
sonian Institution's National Museum of the
American Indian in New York City. He has also
served as the executive director of the Cherokee
National Historical Society in Tahlequah, Okla-
homa, and the Museum of the Cherokee Indian in
Cherokee, North Carolina. Dr. King has written
more than four dozen publications on American
Indian subjects and has taught courses in Chero-
kee studies at the University of Tennessee and
Northeastern State University.

Library of Congress Cataloging in Publication Data
Tribes of the southern woodlands/by the editors
of Time-Life Books.
   p. cm.—(The American Indians)
   Includes bibliographical references and index.
   ISBN 0-8094-9550-3
   ISBN 0-8094-9551-1 (lib. bdg.)
   1. Indians of North America—Southern States—
History. 2. Indians of North America—Southern
States—Social life and customs.
   I. Time-Life Books. II. Series.
E78.S65T75 1994   93-40640
975'.00497-dc20   CIP

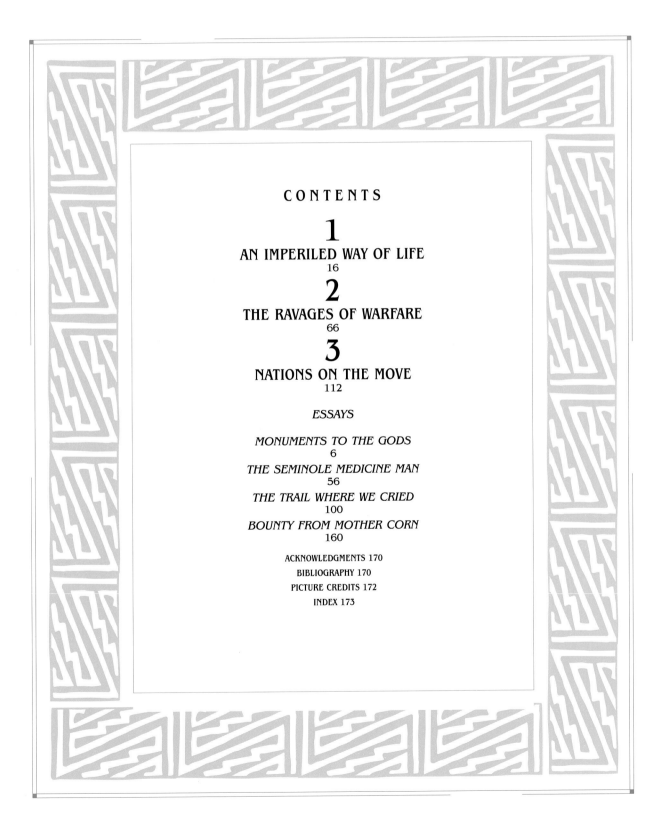

CONTENTS

MONUMENTS TO THE GODS

MACON, GEORGIA.
Nearly 50 feet tall, this flat-topped mound was the foundation for a series of temples, the first erected about AD 900. When a ruler died, his temple was burned, the site covered with earth, and a new building erected for his successor. This cycle continued for some 200 years.

Settling along the major waterways of the south-eastern United States as early as 1500 BC, ancestors of some of the region's most powerful tribes—Choctaw, Chickasaw, Creek, and Seminole—erected massive earthen mounds to thank the gods for the homeland's bountiful resources, the fertile alluvial soil, the rivers teeming with fish, and the dense forests that sheltered abundant game. An entire community might work for decades to build one of these sacred monuments. Many were topped by temples, where divine rulers dwelt and conducted ceremonies on behalf of their people. Some of these temple mounds were also used as burial sites. Effigy mounds fashioned to resemble birds, snakes, and other creatures drawn from Indian religion were meant to be viewed and enjoyed by the gods of the upper world.

In the modern era, many of these sites were destroyed to make way for farms, highways, shopping centers, and office buildings. On these pages are some of the monuments that still remain, silent witnesses to the rich spiritual life of vanished civilizations.

NATCHEZ, MISSISSIPPI. *Named for an emerald-shaped hummock covering almost eight acres, the Emerald Mound complex encompasses several mounds such as the one at right. Early residents of Natchez began erecting the earthen monuments about AD 1300 and used the complex as a ceremonial center for some 300 years.*

EATONTON, GEORGIA. *Measuring 120 feet from wing tip to wing tip, this eagle effigy was created some 1,500 years ago from white quartz boulders found nearby. Extensive damage caused by misguided treasure hunters was repaired during restoration of the site in 1937.*

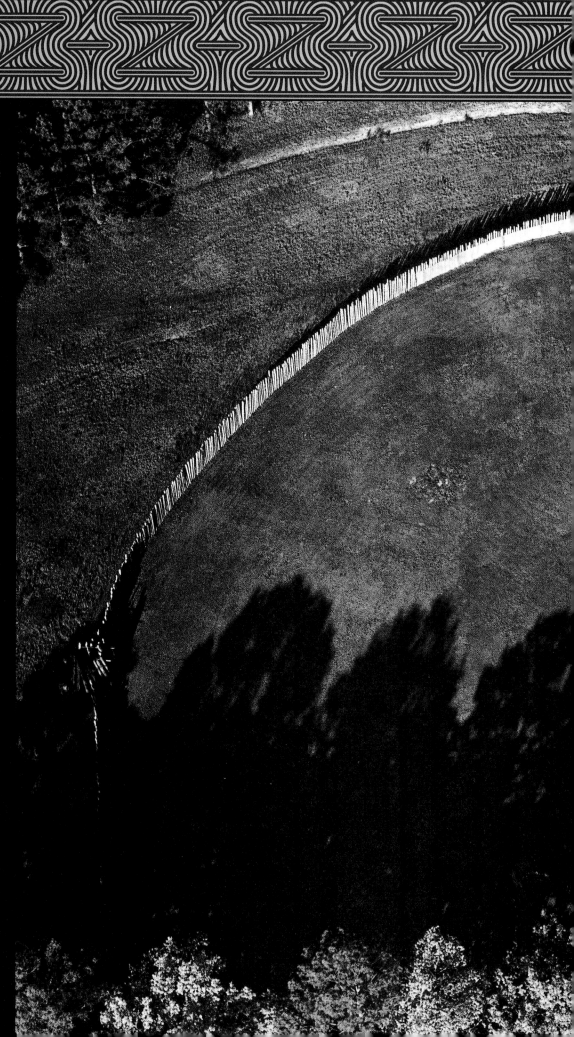

MOUNT GILEAD, NORTH CAROLINA. *At Town Creek Indian Mound, a circular palisade protects a temple elevated on an earthen platform. The small, round structure within the palisade likely would have served as the home of the high priest. The reconstructed site originally flourished as a religious center between 1450 and 1650.*

WINTERVILLE, MISSISSIPPI. *Some 55 feet high, this mound is the largest of several located near Winterville that were built for religious ceremonies some 1,000 years ago. The mound sits adjacent to a farm field that bears the marks of tractor and plow.*

1

AN IMPERILED WAY OF LIFE

Cherokee chief Stalking Turkey, or Cunne Shote, grasps a scalping knife in a portrait painted while he was in London on a peaceful delegation in 1762. Like the other southern woodlands tribes, the Cherokee were eventually devastated by the intrusion of the Europeans with their deadly diseases.

For two months during the winter of 1701, a young Englishman named John Lawson walked and canoed more than 500 miles through the interior of the Carolina Territory. Although newly arrived from London and inexperienced in wilderness travel, Lawson had nevertheless been appointed to make a survey of the area by the True and Absolute Lords Proprietors, the British officials who administered the territory. At the time, only a handful of white men, mostly traders and Spanish explorers, had journeyed into the uncharted hinterland, and little was known of the native peoples who lived there.

Accompanied by Indian guides and a small party of Englishmen, Lawson set out from what he called the "thriving colony" of Charles Towne (now Charleston, South Carolina) and trekked north to the mouth of the Santee River. From there, he moved inland, tracing a horseshoe-shaped route through the vast pine barrens and cane and cypress swamps of the coastal plain into the Piedmont country, and then back again toward the English settlements along Pamlico Sound in present-day North Carolina. Despite the physical difficulties of the trip, Lawson remained an enthusiastic observer, making extensive notes in his journal. "Every step presents some new object," he wrote halfway through the journey, "which still adds invitation to the traveler in these parts."

Lawson was fascinated by the richness and diversity of the plants and wildlife he encountered, from the "endless numbers of panthers, wolves, and other beasts of prey," whose nighttime howling pierced the dark beyond his campsite, to the wild turkeys "several hundred in a gang" that perched in "lofty oaks" so tall that a musket ball could not reach them. He wrote about ducks "of a strange kind, having a red circle about their eyes" and of passenger pigeons in flocks so dense that they sometimes blocked the sun when flying by and "split off the limbs of stout oaks and other trees" when roosting. He found the land to be fertile beyond imagination and teeming with possibilities.

Yet despite all the wonders Lawson discovered among the flora and fauna, his journal, which was later published under the title *A New Voyage to Carolina*, is most remarkable for its description of the native peoples he encountered. On page after page, he painted vivid word portraits of their appearance and customs, which seemed as strange and exotic to him as his European fashions and manners must have appeared to them. "Although their tribes or nations border upon one another," Lawson observed, "yet you may discern as great an alteration in their features and dispositions as you can in their speech, which generally proves quite different from each other, though their nations be not above 10 or 20 miles in distance." He wrote of how some of the Indians grew their fingernails long and how they fixed their hair in bobs on top of the head or tied it back in one long batch that resembled a "horse's tail." He recounted how they greased their bodies with bear fat in order to ward off the cold and insects, and described the manner in which the men decorated their faces with paints made from roots, including a particularly valuable "scarlet root which they get in the hilly country" (probably *Sanguinaria canadensis,* or bloodroot). Prior to going off to war, Lawson noted, the warriors first painted their faces red, and then added a black circle around one eye and a white circle around the other. As a final flourish, they stuck eagle and other bird feathers in their hair.

Whether he came upon them in their hunting camps in the woods or in their large, sometimes palisaded villages, Lawson found Carolina's native peoples to be welcoming and generous. At every settlement, he recounted, he and his companions received offerings of food and shelter (and sometimes female bed partners) for the night. One group of Waxhaw Indians from the Wateree River valley dispatched a messenger to greet Lawson and to encourage him to visit their village, where the people were preparing for a festival. "They laid furs and deer skins upon cane benches for us to sit or lie upon, bringing stewed peaches and green corn, which is a pretty sort of food, and a great increaser of the blood," Lawson noted in his journal. Later that night, the Waxhaw invited him to a feast, held in a large "state house" as "dark as a dungeon, and as hot as one of the Dutch stoves in Holland." While eating from platters of grain, fruit, and bear steak, Lawson watched with fascination as male and female dancers, masked and dressed in feathered costumes, turned "their bodies, arms, and legs into such frightful postures that you would have guessed they had been quite raving mad."

Because of his European prejudices and unfamiliarity with Indian ways, Lawson often misinterpreted or distorted much of what he saw. Nevertheless, his is one of the few early written accounts of the indigenous peoples who once inhabited the Carolina Territory and other regions of the American South. Lawson's journal thus serves as a valuable record of remarkable cultures, most of which have long since vanished. New diseases, spreading colonial settlements, slave raids, and a growing dependence on white men's goods would force the southeastern Indians into a new and precarious existence. Entire nations would be overwhelmed or compelled to leave their ancestral homes and merge with other groups, forming new societies with mixed traditions and blended languages. Many of the old ways and customs would die out and be forgotten. Eventually, by the mid-1800s, most of the native peoples would be removed from the Southeast, driven out by land-hungry whites supported by both the federal and state governments. After undertaking a series of forced emigrations collectively known to history as the Trail of Tears, the Indians would be relocated west of the Mississippi River, where they would attempt to rebuild their shattered lives.

Early clues of the coming catastrophe can be found in Lawson's 1701 journal. Every village he visited, no matter how remote, had already been altered by European contact—from the mixed-blood children playing in the fields to the iron hoes, brass kettles, bottles of rum, and other European goods scattered throughout the households. Even the peaches served by his Waxhaw hosts were introduced by the Spaniards. Yet the biggest—and certainly the most devastating—impact came from particles so minute they were invisible to the naked eye. These were the tiny microbes that the white traders and explorers unwittingly brought into the region and for which, tragically, the Indians lacked immunity. Lawson noted the disastrous effect that the Old World diseases had already had on the Indians. "There is not the sixth savage living within 200 miles of all our settlements, as there were 50 years ago," he wrote, adding that a recent smallpox epidemic had "destroyed whole towns, without leaving one Indian alive."

Still, in 1701, the Indians remained the masters of the Carolina interior and all but a fraction of the lands composing today's American South. Their most ancient forebears had first entered the region—which, in broadest terms, stretches from the Mississippi River eastward to the Atlantic Ocean and from the Gulf of Mexico northward to the Ohio River—at the end of the Ice Age, 10,000 years earlier. They came from the west, drawn by the bountiful plant and animal life. The dense forests, both de-

This stone pipe was carved in the shape of a wildcat by an artisan of the Hopewell culture that flourished about AD 300. A channel drilled through the base served as the pipestem; a bowl in the animal's head held tobacco.

ciduous and pine, and the lush highlands offered a wide variety of game, including deer, elk, bear, wolf, squirrel, raccoon, opossum, otter, turkey, and even alligator in the coastal swamplands. The region also provided an inexhaustible storehouse of seeds, berries, nuts, leaves, and roots. Both freshwater and saltwater fish were also plentiful, including a species of giant catfish that weighed more than 100 pounds.

Although the first southeastern peoples sustained themselves as hunters and gatherers, sometime early in the first millennium AD they began to cultivate corn and other crops. Gradually, as they became more skilled at gardening, they settled into permanent villages and developed a rich culture, characterized by the great earthen mounds they erected as monuments to their gods and as tombs for their distinguished dead. Most of these early mound builders were part of the Adena-Hopewell culture, which had its beginnings near the Ohio River and takes its name from sites in Ohio. The culture spread southward into present-day Louisiana, Alabama, Georgia, and Florida. Its peoples became great traders, bartering jewelry, pottery, animal pelts, tools, and other goods along extensive trading networks that stretched up and down eastern North America and as far west as the Rocky Mountains.

About AD 400, the Hopewell culture fell into decay. Over the next several centuries, it was supplanted by another culture, the Mississippian, named after the river along which many of its earliest villages were located. This complex civilization dominated the Southeast from about AD 700 until shortly before the Europeans began arriving in the 16th century. At the peak of its strength, about the year 1200, it was the most advanced culture in North America. Like their Hopewell predecessors, the Mississippians became highly skilled at growing food, although on a grander scale. They developed an improved strain of corn, which could survive in wet soil and a relatively cool climate, and also learned to cultivate beans. Indeed, agriculture became so important to the Mississippians that it be-

Two rattlesnakes, ornately intertwined, writhe across the sides and bottom of the ceramic vessel at right, made by potters of the late Mississippian culture about AD 1500. In the view at top, the head of one snake appears just below the bottle's mouth, while the other is engraved on its base (bottom view).

came closely associated with the sun—the guarantor of good crops. Many tribes called themselves "children of the sun" and believed their omnipotent priest-chiefs were descendants of the great sun god.

Although most Mississippians lived in small villages or hamlets, many others inhabited large towns with thousands of residents. Most of these huge settlements boasted at least one major flat-topped mound on which stood a temple that contained a sacred flame. Only priests and those charged with guarding the flame could enter the temples. The mounds

also served as ceremonial and trading sites, and at times they were used as burial grounds, although the Mississippians usually built other, smaller mounds for this purpose. Through the later 13th and into the 14th centuries, however, for reasons that remain poorly understood, the great centers of Mississippian culture began to languish and die out.

Even though the Europeans arrived on the continent too late to witness Mississippian culture at its peak, they did find remnants of the great temple mound builders scattered throughout the Southeast. In the spring of 1540, the Spanish conquistador Hernando de Soto came across the Cofitachequi in what is now South Carolina during his bloody three-year march through the American South. A century and a half later, French explorers founding the colony of Louisiana encountered the Natchez living along Saint Catherine Creek near the present-day town in Mississippi that bears their name. Like their Mississippian ancestors, the Natchez had a highly centralized political system and a rich ceremonial life.

The French were particularly struck by the adoration the Indians showed their chief, whom they considered to be a direct descendant of their solar deity. "We set out at two in the afternoon to climb the hill on which the Great Chief's cabin is situated," noted a young Jesuit priest, Father Paul Du Ru, who visited a Natchez village in 1700. "We met him half way there, escorted by the principal personages of the tribe. The chief's manner impresses me; he has the air of an ancient emperor, a long face, sharp eyes, an imperious aquiline nose, a chestnut complexion, and manners somewhat Spanish. The respect with which the other savages approach and serve him is astonishing. If he speaks to one of them, that person thanks him before answering. They never pass in front of him if it can be avoided; if they must, it is with elaborate precautions."

True to their Mississippian heritage, the Natchez had built a large temple on the mound near the chief's house in which they kept an array of sacred objects, including the heads and tails of rattlesnakes, blocks of stone and clay chiseled to depict human beings, stuffed owls, fragments of crystal, and the bones of dead rulers. One sealed wooden box was said to contain the remains of the original sun god, who the Natchez believed had turned himself into stone when he finished his work on earth.

The other powerful Mississippian-style chiefdoms had long since collapsed, weakened by internal tensions and then decimated by the white man's diseases. Within 200 years of first contact with the Europeans, perhaps more than 50 percent of the southeastern Indian population died from smallpox, measles, bubonic plague, and other diseases. Villages vanished and nations crumbled. In many cases, there were barely enough of the living to mourn for the dead. As the Indians perished, so did much of their culture. Disease robbed them of successive generations of elders, causing much of their collected knowledge to vanish overnight. "They have forgot most of their traditions since the establishment of this colony," a Carolina colonist wrote of the Etiwah Indians in 1710, nine years after Lawson's landmark survey. "They keep their festivals and can tell but little of the reasons: Their old men are dead."

As the various tribes began to disintegrate, it became more and more difficult for them to maintain an independent existence. Those peoples who survived joined forces with other groups in new settlements, frequently located far from their traditional homelands. Although the survivors attempted to re-create their old way of life, they usually succeeded in retaining only fragments of past customs and practices. Similar emigrations had occurred among the earlier Mississippian societies, of course, but never on such a massive scale.

The experience of the now extinct Saponi Indians was typical of what befell many of the smaller southeastern tribes. As late as 1670, the Saponi were an independent people living on the Staunton River in Virginia. During the next 50 years, however, they were devastated by disease, and their numbers dwindled to so few that they were no longer able to defend themselves against aggression by neighboring tribes who were their nat-

Framed by thick logs, a passage leads into a reconstructed earthen ceremonial center (above) that was originally built by Indians of the mound builder culture some 1,000 years ago near Macon, Georgia. The interior of such a structure (right) would have been warmed and lighted in ancient times by a fire in the pit at foreground.

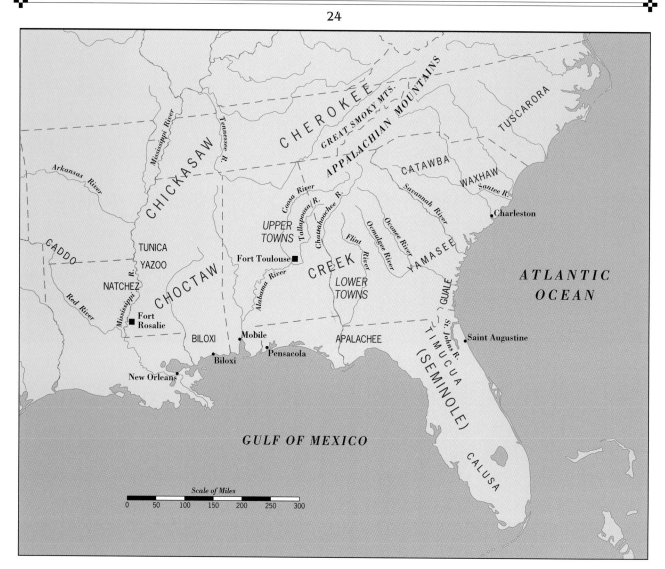

ural enemies. The Saponi were forced to move again and again in search of a safe haven, joining forces first with a succession of similarly hard-pressed tribes before finally migrating to Carolina and becoming part of the Catawba nation. In 1732, still feeling culturally dislocated, many Saponis returned to Virginia. A decade later, they scattered yet again, with the majority of them moving north to present-day New York to become members of the still powerful Iroquois League.

At one time, scores of different tribes representing at least five language groups and countless dialects inhabited the American Southeast, rendering it more linguistically diverse than Europe today. Yet by the middle of the 18th century, most of the tribes had either died out completely or, like the Saponi, merged with larger nations. Four of these larger nations—the Choctaw, Chickasaw, Cherokee, and Creek—came to dominate the political and cultural landscape of the area. Later in the century, they would be joined by a fifth group that would eventually be known as the Seminole. Largely Creek in origin, the Seminole peoples emigrated to Florida and began to assume a distinct identity as they adapted to a tropi-

From the mist-shrouded valleys of the Appalachians to the vast swamps of Florida, the South-east was once home to perhaps 100 tribes, but few sur-vived European dis-ease and coloniza-tion. Shown here are some of the peo-ples that figure prominently in this tragedy—from those who are now no more than names to the nations that en-dure to this day.

A sacred staff of the Chickasaw tribe bears delicate carvings of ears of corn. According to legend, a similar staff was carried during the tribe's migration from the west. Imbued with spirit power, it pointed the way to a new home for the tribe in what is today northern Mississippi.

cal environment. Although many other sizable Indian nations existed in the region—the Catawba in South Carolina, the Yuchi in Georgia, and the Tunica-Biloxi in Mississippi, for example—their influence never approached that of the five principal nations.

The Choctaw inhabited the rolling, forested hills of present-day southern Mississippi, western Alabama, and eastern Louisiana. According to one of their oral traditions shared with the Chickasaw, their ancestors crossed the Mississippi River from some long-forgotten land in the west. The Choctaw were led on this journey, as legend has it, by a white dog aided by the mysterious leanings of a sacred staff. Each evening, Chacta, the Choctaw culture hero, stuck the staff into the ground, and each morning found it tilting to the east. The white dog then led them in the direction of the rising sun until one morning Chacta discovered that the dog had died and the staff was standing upright. That was where he decided to settle and where, in celebration, the Choctaw built the *nanih waiya*, or "leaning mound." It would be the site of their political and religious gatherings for centuries to come, until a final council meeting in the early 1800s. The mound can still be seen in a field near the town of Philadelphia in east-central Mississippi.

To the north of the Choctaw, in what are now the Tombigbee highlands of northern Mississippi, lay the heartland of the Chickasaw, a small but powerful tribe renowned for the ferocity of its warriors. "In a long chase they will stretch away, through the rough woods, by the bare track, for two or three hundred miles, in pursuit of a lying enemy, with the continued speed, and eagerness, of a staunch pack of blood hounds, till they shed blood," wrote James Adair, a British trader who lived among the Chickasaw during the 18th century. The close cultural and language similarities between the Chickasaw and the Choctaw indicate that the two groups were probably once a single people. Several Chickasaw legends support this theory, for they tell of how two brothers, Chacta and Chicsa, jointly led their tribe to the eastern forests and then decided that the people should split into two groups occupying adjoining homelands, an arrangement that in time spawned a bitter rivalry.

With a population of only about 5,000 in 1700, the Chickasaw never approached the size of the Choctaw, who during the same time numbered about 21,000. Yet despite their small numbers, the Chickasaw laid claim to a broad swath of territory that extended north across western Tennessee and Kentucky to the Ohio River and east into Alabama. They commanded a long stretch of the Mississippi River, the Father of Waters, controlling the river traffic and much of the flow of trade goods between the West and the tribes of the Southeast.

Well to the east of the Chickasaw, in the low mountains and rich river valleys of the southern Appalachians, lived the Cherokee, a name that most likely derived from either the Choctaw word *chiluk-ki,* meaning "cave people," or the Muskogean word *tciloki,* meaning "people of a different speech." The Cherokee, however, called themselves *aniyunwiya,* or the "principal people," and believed that their homeland stood at the center of the physical world. Unlike the other major nations of the Southeast, who all spoke dialects of Muskogean, the Cherokee spoke Iroquoian, the language of their northeastern kin. Archaeological evidence suggests that they first settled in the Great Smoky Mountains of present-day western North Carolina, and then spread as far as the western tip of Virginia's Blue Ridge, into eastern Tennessee, and south into the hill country of South Carolina, Alabama, and Georgia.

Still farther south, across the remainder of Alabama and Georgia, dwelt dozens of smaller tribes that were known to the British in the late 17th century as Creeks. While these tribes were generally autonomous, they were also part of a larger, multitribal alliance that predated the Europeans. Generally speaking, it consisted of two large regional groups of villages, which the Carolina traders referred to as Upper and Lower Creeks. The upper towns were located in the Tallapoosa, Coosa, and upper Alabama River valleys and the lower towns in the Chattahoochee and Flint River systems. These groupings were obvious to late-17th-century French and Spanish traders as well, who called the Upper Creeks Tallapoosas, and the Lower Creeks Cowetas, after two of the principal towns.

The Creeks had no single tongue. Among the Indians living along one six-mile stretch of the Alabama River, for example, James Adair noted seven distinct languages being spoken. So different were these languages that another British trader, Timothy Barnard, who had learned to speak the Creek languages of Muskogee and Hitchiti fluently, claimed he could never gain more than a superficial understanding of Yuchi, even after marrying a Yuchi woman.

It was once thought that the British chose the word "Creek" because southeastern Indians built their villages above the banks of rivers and streams. Many scholars now believe, however, that the name was first used to describe a specific group of Muskogee speakers, the Ochesee, who at the time of the founding of Charles Towne in 1670 lived in present-day Georgia along a stretch of the upper Ocmulgee River that the traders

An ancient earthen mound in Mississippi called "nanih waiya," sacred to the Choctaw, rises beyond a cornfield in a 1914 photograph. According to one Choctaw origination legend, the initial members of the tribe ascended from a watery underworld to be born from the mound, drying themselves on its sunny flanks.

called Ochesee Creek. The traders who stopped at the villages to barter for deerskins referred to the Indians there as Ochesee Creeks—or, eventually, just Creeks. The name stuck and followed the Ochesee when they were forced to move farther west with several other tribes to the banks of the Chattahoochee River some 50 years later.

Soon the British were calling all of the Indians living along the Chattahoochee and the other neighboring rivers Creeks. Gradually the Indians themselves came to accept the name, if only to make it easier to deal with the whites. In the early 18th century, leaders of the various Creek tribes formed a national council to talk about common concerns and present a unified front against the whites. When the British came to understand the council's influence over the multiplicity of more or less autonomous towns, they labeled the Creek domain a confederacy. Because of its large population, stalwart warriors, and skillful diplomats, the Creek Confederacy became the most formidable Indian group in the Southeast.

Despite their differences of ancestry and language, the southeastern Indian tribes shared a large number of social and cultural traits. All of them lived in chiefdoms, or towns, usually in houses erected on the banks of a river or stream, close to the fertile bottom land where they planted their crops. The larger towns extended into the woods for several miles, connected by a winding network of trails. Each town was built around a central plaza, or commons, which functioned as the ceremonial center for the community. The plaza typically had three components: a *tcokofa,* or circu-

Shown here and on the following pages are portraits of Creeks, Choctaws, Cherokees, Chickasaws, and Seminoles who once dominated the southern woodlands from Florida and the Carolinas to the banks of the Mississippi River. The photographs were made in the 19th and early 20th centuries.

SEMINOLE MOTHER AND DAUGHTER, ABOUT 1919

lar town house; a summer council house; and a flat, cleared field for ball games and ceremonies.

The tightly constructed tcokofa served as the wintertime meeting place for the town council and also as the site of certain celebrations (such as the one John Lawson attended with the Waxhaw). It also functioned as a guesthouse for visitors with no local kin and as a shelter for elderly members of the tribe who had no relatives to care for them. A typical tcokofa measured about 25 feet in diameter, with the highest point of the domed ceiling approximately 25 feet above the ground. One particularly large Cherokee rotunda, however, was said to accommodate 500 people. The inside walls were lined with benches, about seven feet wide and seven feet long, which were covered by cane mats. Some of the larger town houses might have two or even three tiers of benches. As the buildings had only two sources of ventilation—a small smoke hole in the roof for the fire and the low entryway—they were exceedingly dark and musty, but retained heat extremely well.

The summer council house was not a single building, but a number of separate, rectangular shedlike structures, each about 30 feet in length, with open fronts, wattle-and-daub walls, and a canopy of leaves and brush woven or thatched together. The sheds faced each other in an open square, which covered about half an acre, and were frequently aligned in the four cardinal directions. In the middle of the square burned the sacred fire. Like the town house, the walls of the sheds were lined with benches, or "beds," as the Creek called them. Low partitions of dried clay divided each shed into compartments, each one belonging to one or more clans, who often decorated their section with clan symbols and various ritual objects such as eagle feathers, swan wings, medicinal herbs, scalping knives, or war clubs. The town elders were given honored seats in the front on the beds facing the square.

The third component of the central plaza was the chunky yard, a clearing about 100 yards or more square, surrounded on two or more sides by a low earthen wall. As its name implies, the townspeople used the space to play a ball game called chunky. Although there were variations to

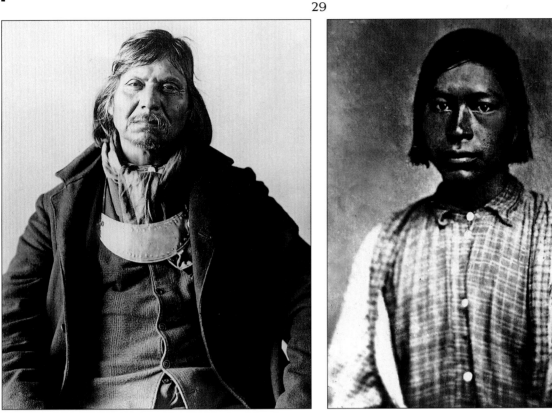

A CHIEF OF THE CREEKS, 1901   YOUNG CHICKASAW BOY, MID-19TH CENTURY

the game, it generally involved a player rolling a round stone along the ground and attempting to throw a stick at the spot where he guessed that the stone would stop. A tall post used for another kind of ball game that women as well as men could play often stood in the center of the yard. Shorter posts, sometimes adorned with the scalps and skulls of slain enemies, might be placed in the corners of the yard. They were used for tying up and torturing war captives.

The public buildings of the central plaza were surrounded by family homes, neatly laid out in rectangular blocks. Southeastern households tended to be large, containing a husband and wife, their children, one or more sons-in-law, a number of grandchildren as well as a few aged dependents, and perhaps a few orphans and adopted war captives.

Most southeastern households were matrilocal, grouped in clan communities related through the mother's clan. Each household utilized a cluster of buildings—a summer house, a winter house, and perhaps one or two storage sheds, depending on the wealth of the family. The winter house was round, like the public town house, with the floor dug several feet below the surface of the ground. It was heavily insulated with a combination of clay and dried grass or Spanish moss. A small entryway, L-shaped to keep out the draft, was the only opening. Raised sleeping benches lined the wall at a level just high enough, in the words of one English visitor, so that a "flea could not reach them in one jump." These hive-like structures were so well insulated that a few coals were all that was

CHEROKEE NAMED CLIMBING BEAR, 1888

GRANNY SPOT, CREEK WOMAN WITH MONOCLE, 1900

needed to keep the occupants warm and snug, even on the bitterest winter night. "Their cabins are round and vaulted," wrote Father Jacques Gravier, a French missionary who traveled among the Tunica Indians of present-day western Mississippi in November of 1700. "They are lathed with canes and plastered with mud from bottom to top, within and without, with a good covering of straw. There is no light except by the door, and no matter how little fire there is (the smoke of which has no escape but the door), it is as hot as a vapor bath. At night a lighted torch of dried canes serves as a candle and keeps all the cabin warm."

The Indians built their summer homes on frameworks of notched, rot-resistant posts, interwoven with saplings and tied together with reeds or branches. Each house consisted of a single rectangular room covered by a gabled roof that was shingled with cypress or pine bark and weighted down by logs. Some summer homes stood two stories high. The ends of the gables were frequently left open to allow fresh breezes to blow through. Others were sealed to keep out annoying insects. In addition to the summer and winter homes, each household commonly built an assemblage of smaller buildings, which were used for storage and cooking, as well as a special temporary hut for women to live in during their menstrual periods. The women also gave birth there, remaining in seclusion until their babies were about four months old.

In semitropical coastal areas, the Indians often built houses on stilts for protection against dampness and snakes. Called a *chickee* by the Semi-

CHOCTAW BALLPLAYER WITH RACKET, ABOUT 1860

WALINI, A CHEROKEE WOMAN, 1887

noles, this kind of shelter lacked walls and had a roof made of palmetto leaves, from which canopies could be lowered at night as protection against mosquitoes and heavy dew.

The southeastern system of government was designed to promote communal harmony. Each town had one principal official called a *miko,* a Muskogean word meaning "civil chief." (The Cherokee referred to the person holding this office as *uku.*) In contrast to the absolute power of the Mississippian rulers, the authority of an 18th-century miko was limited to receiving visiting dignitaries, overseeing the public granary, initiating certain feasts, and serving as the executive officer of the council, the town's central political body. He governed by persuasion, not coercion, and was traditionally associated with peace.

The town council functioned as an open and democratic forum. Here decisions of daily importance regarding food, shelter, and family were made. Typically towns formed themselves into alliances, from those consisting of just a few towns to those embracing an entire nation. It was at this higher level of government that major debates on war, peace, and trade were most often conducted.

Like the miko, the town council possessed no coercive powers. Rather, its members strove in their decision-making process to achieve consensus while avoiding direct confrontation. Everyone was allowed to speak his piece without interruption; if a council member disapproved of someone else's argument, he often simply remained silent.

JACK TIGERTAIL, SEMINOLE, 1917

QUALLA, A CHEROKEE WOMAN

The town's warriors constituted one of the most influential blocks of council members. The Creek model was typical. The Creek tribes recognized three grades of warriors: war chiefs, big warriors, and little warriors, based on their battlefield deeds. One of the war chiefs was always designated as the town's *tastanagi tako,* a Muskogean word for "great warrior." It was the duty of the man holding this title to lead the town in times of war. Men who had not yet proved themselves in combat also sat in council but ranked below the warriors.

A group called the second men made up another important body of members. These individuals were associated with the miko and were responsible for the town's internal affairs, supervising such activities as building houses, maintaining the square ground, and cultivating the communal gardens. The beloved old men, esteemed elders who had won special honors in their younger days and were now valued for their wisdom, filled advisory positions. Two additional officials were the *yatika,* or "interpreter," and the *holibonaya,* or "war speaker." The interpreter delivered the miko's speeches so that the civil chief might avoid direct confrontation with anyone opposing his ideas. The war speaker, the town's most eloquent orator, represented the views of the great warrior.

Before beginning a council meeting, the members smoked sacred tobacco and purged their bodies of pollution by drinking a ritual tea made from the dried leaves and twigs of the holly shrub, *Ilex vomitoria.* Although the Indians themselves called it "white drink" because it symbolized puri-

CREEK MAN, ABOUT 1880

ty, the beverage is known today as "black drink," the name the Europeans gave it because of its color. The second men were charged with the responsibility of preparing black drink, which was made in a manner similar to tea. The Indians first roasted the dried leaves and twigs and then boiled them in water until the liquid turned dark brown. Medicine men sometimes blew into it with a cane straw for hours in order to evoke its sacred powers. Normally served in large conch shells, the caffeine-rich brew was considered ready to drink when it was no longer scalding. Black drink acted as both a stimulant and a diuretic, and sometimes, for reasons that are not well understood, as an emetic. Council meetings were not the only occasion for consuming black drink, however. The Indians drank it informally and before every important undertaking, often in great quantities. When consumed ceremonially, it was deliberately vomited up as part of a purification process.

The many towns of the Creek Confederacy belonged to one of two sides, or "fires," marked by the color red or white. The Creeks referred to members of their own fire as *anhissi,* or "my friend," and to members of the opposing fire as *ankipaya,* or "my enemy." Each summer, red towns and white towns competed against each other in a special ball game, called "match play" by the English, involving teams with scores of players, each one carrying two ball sticks. The numbers of people engaged were sometimes so large that games were often held on the open expanses of dry flood plains. Each side had its own goal consisting of two posts and a crossbar. To score a point, a player could either put the ball through his own goal or cause it to strike any part of the goalpost.

Preparations for a game involved days of ritual observances, and during the contest, entire towns worked themselves into a frenzy of cheering, heckling, and gambling on the outcome. Although a given town could challenge any town of the opposite fire, most had a favorite rival they competed against. Much was at stake. For young men of both sides, the game was a chance to gain honor in an arena other than the battlefield. The prestige of a town hung in the balance as well. A town that lost the annual summer match game three times in a row was often required to convert to the winner's side. Thus, white towns might become red towns, and vice versa. Although the change of name meant little in a practical sense,

STRUCTURES OF A CHEROKEE VILLAGE

In the early 18th century, some 60 to 80 Cherokee villages dotted the tribe's homelands in Tennessee, Georgia, and North Carolina. From 200 to 400 or more people lived in a village, which consisted of individual dwellings scattered around a town center. Based on the descriptions of contemporary travelers as well as modern archaeological excavations, the drawings below and on the following pages portray the structures of a typical Cherokee settlement about 1700.

Cherokees lived in two kinds of houses: a summer house, generally used by a single extended family, and an adjacent winter house, which might be shared by two or more families. In addition, many households kept a small raised building used for storing corn (far right).

A circular building with a cone-shaped thatched roof, the winter house, or hothouse (left), where villagers lived and slept during cold weather, was kept so warm that the Indians stripped down

to breechcloths or skirts upon entering it. Indeed, thanks to its thick walls—plastered with six or seven inches of clay and vegetation—and the fire that burned continuously at its center, the dwelling could attain temperatures in excess of 80 degrees. When the need arose, medicine men would visit the houses and make steam baths from herbal brews to heal the sick, or to cleanse and purify the occupants in preparation for rituals. And, as depicted here, wise men frequently visited to re-gale the occupants with exemplary tales and oft-told legends.

Rectangular in shape with thin wattle-and-daub walls and a gabled roof of bark shingles that were held in place by saplings, the Cherokee summer house (right) may have provided year-round storage for a family's food and possessions, as well as serving as warm-weather sleeping quarters. In addition, the shelter was used for a variety of other activities, including mending and weaving, and cleaning weapons.

PLAZA AND PAVILIONS

According to Cherokee tradition, all inhabitants of a village usually lived within a drumbeat's call of the square ground, an open-air plaza located at the center of town. Used during warm weather for dances, seasonal celebrations, and recreational activities, the square covered about half an acre. It was customarily surrounded by seven pavilions—one for each of the seven clans of the tribe—which were fitted with tiers of benches. During events held at the square, the villagers sat with their respective clans.

In addition, the square ground sometimes served as a sports arena. Especially popular among the Cherokee was stickball, an intensely competitive game steeped in ritual. In the drawing at right, two teams face off before the beginning of a contest. Behind them are the rough-cut saplings used as goalposts.

THE TOWN COUNCIL HOUSE

During the cold months, community gatherings in a Cherokee village moved indoors to the town council house, which stood adjacent to the square ground. Constructed with the same thick clay walls as a winter dwelling, a council house commonly measured from 25 to 50 feet in diameter; the largest could accommodate between 400 and 500 people. Tiered benches along the walls surrounded a central open area where a sacred fire burned. Traditionally the structure had eight sides: one for the entrance and seven others to correspond to the seven clans of the Cherokee tribe.

The council house served as both temple and public hall, a place for religious rites as well as political meetings and a variety of other events, such as ceremonial and social dancing. People sat according to rank, with the seats behind the fire reserved for the leaders and so-called beloved men or women, and the clan members grouped in designated sections.

Warm inside on even the coldest days, the town council house was also used to lodge travelers, as well as the old men and women of the village who had no relatives to take them in and care for them. In the rendering here, the town chief is shown directing preparations for an event, wearing his traditional turkey-feather cloak and headdress made of feathers dyed yellow.

CHIEF'S HEADDRESS

the symbolic conquering that it signified brought intense humiliation to the defeated town and pride to the victorious.

Much more important than the town to the life of a southeastern Indian was the clan. Indeed, clan ties were as strong as those of a family. Clan affiliations provided a man or woman with a sense of belonging and responsibility, with a role to play as a member of the community. Clans functioned as both police and courts, and clan kin could always be counted on for assistance in times of need.

The origins of the clans were rooted in ancient times, when the belief evolved that people were descended from spirit beings that could take the form of anything in the natural world. Clans were formed of people who claimed descent from a common ancestor, which could be an animal, a bird, a fish, a reptile, a vegetable, or even a force of nature. Among the numerous Creek clans were the deer, bear, beaver, alligator, panther, raccoon, wolf, wild potato, eagle, turkey, and supernatural beings called wind people. Like their towns, Creek clans were either red or white, and depending on their color, they traditionally provided certain types of community leaders. Mikos and second men were generally from white clans, for example; great warriors were from red.

All southeastern clans were matrilineal; that is, children automatically became members of their mothers' clans. Thus a girl would learn cooking, basket weaving, gardening, and other female duties from her mother and her mother's sisters, but a boy would turn to his mother's brothers, rather

*Wearing the tradi-
tional loincloth, a
Creek ballplayer,
circa 1910, holds a
pair of rackets used
in the form of
lacrosse played by
the Indians of the
Southeast since an-
cient times. The
rackets, like the
Choctaw ones
shown below, left,
were fashioned of
leather thongs and
wood that was bent
into a loop at one
end to form a ball-
catching pocket.*

than to his father, for instruction in male skills, such as hunting, fighting, and proper ritual behavior.

Most clans held meetings every fall. On these occasions, clan elders recited family history and gave recognition to members who had brought honor to the clan during the previous year. Individuals whose behavior dishonored the clan were also mentioned—an act of public humiliation that served to keep younger members in line.

Marriage within one's clan was considered incest and thus severely punished, frequently by death. A man and woman of different clans, how-ever, could marry simply by having an exchange of gifts between their families. Proposals were often accomplished indirectly. A young Choctaw man, for example, would propose to a girl by furtively tossing a small stick or pebble at her feet. If the girl threw the item back, he knew she had ac-cepted his offer. Most communities acknowledged a marriage with a feast and celebration for the whole town. The newlyweds would then set up their household with the bride's family, either in the house of her parents or in a separate dwelling nearby.

Although divorce was not infrequent, marriage was taken seriously and infidelity strongly condemned. Punishment for unfaithfulness was de-termined by the clan and could be severe, especially for women. Penalties included public head shavings or whippings, the clipping of an ear or nose, and even permanent exile. Divorce, like marriage, was a relatively uncom-plicated matter. A Cherokee woman, who by tribal law owned her family's house and property, could declare herself divorced simply by placing a bundle of her husband's belongings outside their dwelling. He would then move back into his mother's house, or into the home of another wife, if he happened to have more than one.

Some tribes allowed men to have multiple wives, usually sisters or maternal cousins of the first wife and thus members of the same clan. The trader James Adair reported that Chickasaw men could marry as many wives as they could support and that many of them ridiculed white men for preferring a single spouse. The practice of polygamy, however, appears to have been extended only to men; southeastern women were generally expected to remain faithful to one husband.

Everyone in the village, from the youngest to the oldest, worked hard to support their extended families and to contribute to the prosperity of the larger community. Daily and seasonal chores were divided according to gender. The men felled trees and cleared fields for planting, hunted and fished, repaired tools and weapons, built houses and other town structures, and organized ball games and religious ceremonies. It was customary for them to spend many weeks away from home, either on raids against enemies or on friendly visits to other towns. The women cared for the children and the homes, cultivated crops, prepared, cooked, and preserved food, gathered wild foodstuffs and firewood, and made the clothing, baskets, pottery, and other household items. On occasion, women were asked to accompany the men of the tribe to the battlefield, where they provided a kind of running commentary—in song—on the ebb and flow of the fighting. "The Chickasaws usually carry 10 or 12 young women with them to the wars, whose business is to sing a fine tune, during any action," explained one Carolina colonist. "If their own men succeed, they praise them highly and degrade the enemy, but if they give back, the singers alter their praises into reproaches, thus changing notes according as their party advances or gives way."

Not all activities were restricted by gender, however. Both women and men participated in the most important religious event of the year, the annual Busk, or Green Corn Ceremony. Throughout this four- to eight-day festival, held every summer when the corn ripened, the southeastern people celebrated the year's harvest and offered thanks to the sun god and the great corn spirit. It was both a solemn and joyous occasion, a time of renewal and forgiveness. As part of the event, the women cleaned all the houses and public buildings in the town, throwing away broken pottery and tools and disposing of any leftover food. They also extinguished all fires, and then lit the sacred fire in the square ground. The men, meanwhile, imbibed black drink and fasted before gathering in the square ground to resolve grudges and forgive old debts and all crimes, except murder. In addition, they submitted to ritual scratching with sharpened sticks, offering up their blood as another means of purification.

Unhappy marriages were officially dissolved at this meeting, and couples who had eloped against the wishes of their families were welcomed back into the

Arrayed for athletic combat, a modern Creek ballplayer wears his village's red uniform with his "tails"—made of plaited material rather than horsehair—hanging at his sides. Indian teams still maintain the age-old tradition of the ball game.

Running full tilt, Choctaw players speed down a cleared ball field in a photograph taken in the 1980s. Today's teams are generally much smaller than those with hundreds of players that once charged up and down huge fields that sometimes measured 300 yards in length.

community. The festival ended with a feast, during which the first corn of the season was eaten. The yatika would rise and speak of the miko's desire for the people to be filled with the spirit of peace and generosity during the coming year. If visitors from other tribes were present at the celebration, a peace pipe might be passed around. After the feast, women took embers from the sacred fire back to their homes to light their families' hearths for the new year.

Yet despite all the talk of peace at the annual Green Corn Ceremony, war was very much a part of southeastern life. The men referred to war in terms that could be translated as "beloved occupation," and looked upon it as the way to achieve glory and status within the community.

The impetus for most of the combat was revenge. The Indians believed that if one person killed another, the slain person's spirit could not go on to the "darkening land"—the place where people dwelt after death—unless the death was avenged. This task was the responsibility of members of the victim's clan. Once vengeance was achieved, the soul of the victim was free to travel to the nether world, and the sorrow of those who were grieving for the slain person was relieved. The death of the killer, or of one of his clansmen, usually ended the matter. When a different tribe was involved, however, the conflict could escalate to full-scale war, and many deaths might result.

Initially, the Europeans were slow to comprehend the Indian principle of retaliation. If a European murdered an Indian, for example, the victim's entire tribe would hold all colonists responsible and declare war against all of them. But if an Indian killed a colonist, the Europeans, rather than blame the whole tribe, normally demanded only that the killer be handed over, a Western concept of justice that the Indians found completely incomprehensible. Later in the 18th century, however, the Europeans frequently adopted an Indian version of collective responsibility when it came time for exacting revenge for the killing of whites.

Among the Indians, blood was not always avenged with equal blood. Often the killer's clan would send peace envoys to talk with the clan of the murdered individual. They might insist that the action had been unsanctioned by their council and that the guilty party was rash and inexperienced. Sometimes the council representing the victim agreed to accept compensation, typically in the form of slaves or captives, and that ended the conflict. Other times, however, the clan leader might demand revenge. If the conflict involved an entire town, the community's war chief might argue for full-scale combat, and if he could attract a sufficient number of volunteers, the town declared war by displaying a war club painted red or by flying a red flag for all to see.

Warfare among the southeastern tribes tended to be seasonal. War parties, normally numbering no more than 40 men, ventured out in the late spring, summer, or early fall. Territorial gain was rarely an Indian objective. Rather, the goal was to kill or capture a number of the enemy while suffering the fewest possible casualties among one's own tribesmen. Attacks were normally launched from ambush or at night while the enemy slept. The war party frequently announced its arrival by setting fire to an enemy house and falling upon the occupants as they fled the flames. Knives and clubs were the weapons of choice because they had to be used at close range and required greater courage than bows and arrows. When possible, the attackers took the scalps or entire heads of their enemies back to their towns as trophies. The scalps were sometimes affixed to the boughs of pine trees, which were thought to suppress any lingering evil, or they might be placed on the roofs of the winter houses of the persons whose deaths had been avenged to appease their souls. To terrorize their foes,

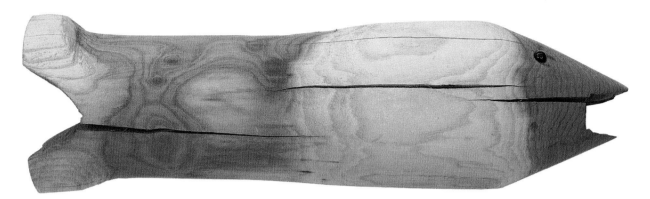

This carved wooden fish was placed atop a tall pole to serve as a target in a popular Indian pastime called pole game. Female players hurled a ball with their hands to knock the target down; men and boys were required to fling the ball with their ball sticks.

A kneeling man, part of a tobacco pipe dating from the Mississippian era, was carved to represent a player of the age-old southeastern game called chunky. The figure prepares to roll a special smooth stone, at which other players launched wooden javelins.

the Timucua of northern Florida dismembered their victims' bodies and hung the limbs on trees outside their towns.

Warriors often returned with live captives, whose fates varied considerably. Children and female prisoners were usually adopted by their captor's clan and eventually treated like any other kin. Men received less kindly treatment. They either became a slave of the warrior who had captured them or were tortured to death. Although a slave performed menial tasks, such as collecting firewood and tanning deer hides, his main value seems to have been to confer status on his owner. In fact, Indian slave owners placed few physical demands on their *ati nahsa'i,* or the "ones who are owned." As James Adair dryly noted of the Cherokee, "Their slaves are not over-burdened with work." Most slaves were allowed freedom of movement within their captor's town. To escape, however, was almost impossible; it was the widespread practice of Indian masters to maim the feet of their slaves to prevent flight. Although few attempted to escape, all must have wished they could, for a slave led a precarious life. Having no clan kin or allies, he could be bartered or put to death at any time.

Most male captives, particularly older ones who were known to have achieved many war honors, were condemned to ritualistic torture soon after they were brought back from a raid. Stripped naked and tied to a wooden pole or frame, the victims were first beaten and then tormented with fire. Women customarily inflicted the torture, singing songs of retribution while they did so. The prisoner was expected to sing his own defiant death song for as long as he remained conscious. If he showed fear, the onlookers roared with laughter and taunted him further. Sometimes the torture went on for several days before the victim finally succumbed. His scalp was then given to the family whose slain relative the torture had avenged to "wipe the tears from their eyes." Afterward, his body was cut up into pieces so it would not be whole in the afterworld.

The practice of slavery assumed a new—and devastating—dimension with the arrival of the Europeans. Indeed, with the exception of the spread of disease, the enslavement of Indians by the newcomers to the continent had the most destructive effect on the lives of native peoples in the South-

Early French colonizers look on as a group of Florida's Timucua Indians brew, consume, and then spew out the so-called black drink in this 16th-century engraving. Black drink was employed by many southeastern tribes in the course of purification rites.

east. From the time the gold-seeking Spanish explorer Juan Ponce de León first stepped ashore in 1513 on the land he called Florida, Europeans assumed it was their natural right to kidnap Indians and force them to work as guides, translators, and bearers for their expeditions in the New World, or to abduct and transport them to other colonies for slave labor.

In the beginning, the Native Americans were caught unawares. At the time that two Spanish caravels landed near the Savannah River in 1521, the Cusabo Indians welcomed the strangers who stepped off the ships into their midst. They showered the Spaniards with gifts and expressed admiration for their beards and woolen and silk clothing. "But what then!" exclaimed Pietro Martire d' Anghiera, a Spaniard and historian for the Catholic Church who chronicled the exploration of the Americas. "The Spaniards ended by violating this hospitality. For when they had finished their explorations, they enticed numerous natives by lies and tricks to visit their ships, and when the vessels were quickly crowded with men and women, they raised anchor, set sail, and carried these despairing unfortunates into slavery. By such means they sowed hatred and warfare throughout the pleasant and peaceful region, separating children from their parents and wives from husbands."

From cruel incidents such as this, the Indians learned to distrust the bearded men who came to their land from across the sea. They also began to strike back at the intruders. That same year, 1521, native warriors mortally wounded Ponce de León during his unsuccessful attempt to establish a permanent Spanish settlement in Florida.

During the 50 years following Ponce de León's death, a succession of conquistadors, including Hernando de Soto, made forays into the Southeast, aimed more at plunder than at colonization. In 1564 a group of French Protestant reformers known as the Huguenots established what might have become a successful settlement at the mouth of the Saint Johns River in northern Florida. But the Spaniards drove them out the following year as the opening move in a campaign to secure Florida in order to protect the routes of their treasure fleets. Shortly thereafter, Spain began building outposts along the Atlantic and Gulf coasts, forts in nearly every harbor, and missions as far north as Virginia. All but those in Florida and southeastern Georgia eventually failed, however, and the Spaniards settled back to pacify the Indians living near their capital at Saint Augustine in northeastern Florida.

The first governor of the Florida territory, Pedro Menéndez de Avilés, wanted to "tame" the Indians with fire and sword, but he was overruled by

church and king, who advocated a policy that combined ruthlessness with largess, along with a heavy dose of missionary proselytizing. As elsewhere in New Spain, the Spaniards marked the Indians not for extermination but for transformation into loyal subjects of His Most Catholic Majesty. At first, the Spaniards encouraged marriages between Spanish men and Indian women and even the exchange of children between Spanish nobles and high-ranking Indians. But most of the Indians were reduced to a laboring class, subject to Spanish whims, and were forced by the missionaries to give up age-old customs such as the practice of polygamy. Many of them resisted, and a few even rose up in open rebellion. In 1597, for example, the Guale Indians in the northeast corner of the colony revolted, killing five Franciscan friars.

Two Seminole women wearing traditional patchwork clothing care for children in an open-sided hut called a chickee. Well adapted to Florida's subtropical climate, chickees were fashioned of pine or cypress timbers with roofs of thatched palmetto fronds secured by logs, as shown in the late-19th-century engraving at right.

In time, however, the Spaniards stabilized Florida by establishing separate Indian and Spanish republics that were united in their allegiance to crown and church. Whereas Saint Augustine remained the sole Spanish municipality, the Indian republic contained some 40 towns with a total population of about 26,000 Christian Indians. It was divided into three provinces named after the dominant tribe of each region: Guale on the Georgia coast, Timucua in central Florida, and Apalachee near the modern city of Tallahassee. Although the Spaniards posted a small body of troops in each province, they allowed the Indians to govern themselves largely as they always had, except for the presence of priests and the requirement that they set aside a portion of their produce to pay taxes and support the church. In some instances, the town chiefs and the Spanish governor enjoyed mutually beneficial relationships, respecting each other's power and authority. Aided by the introduction of European agricultural techniques and tools as well as livestock, the Indian republic often produced food surpluses that helped feed Spanish colonies in the Caribbean and elsewhere.

While the Spaniards were establishing themselves in Florida, the French were busy expanding their empire down the Mississippi River. Na-

Amoneeta Sequoya, a Cherokee shown here at age 68, was tutored in the medicine man tradition. He was a popular healer who ministered to Indians and whites alike.

CHEROKEE HEALING

European explorers in the Southeast marveled at Indian medicine men, who, relying mainly on plants, treated patients with a skill that seemed unsurpassed by Old World doctors. Of such Cherokee healers, one Englishman wrote, "They have a great knowledge in applying herbs and plants, and seldom if ever fail to effect a thorough cure."

According to a Cherokee legend, human diseases were devised by animals who had grown weary of human cruelty. Plants, friendly to humans, created cures for each disease. The healer's task was to determine which animal his patient had offended and then concoct a cure from the correct plant. A disease caused by an angry rabbit spirit, for example, called for "rabbit food," also known as wild roses.

The intrinsic properties of many plants made them potent cures. Some were less effective but, when added to the healer's entreaties to the spirits, at least comforted the patients until they recovered or succumbed to their illness.

Although their numbers are small, Cherokee healers in North Carolina and Oklahoma continue to practice the medicine of their forefathers, keeping herbal lore alive for future generations.

Written in Cherokee is a prescription for curing an ailment. Each Indian healer kept a private book of medicine rituals with notes about the curative powers of various plants and incantations.

Among the healing plants in this medicine man's bundle are grapevines, elm leaves, sassafras root, cedar chips, and cockleburs. To test his selections, a healer tied the material into a packet and threw it into a river. Worthless remedies sank, but good ones floated.

Masks such as this were worn during ceremonies conducted to ensure the well-being of the community at large.

To forecast the course of disease, healers caught the first rays of the sun with crystals such as the one at left. Brilliance meant the outlook was favorable; a cloudy crystal portended death.

tive peoples watched as a small but steady stream of explorers, including Louis Joliet, Jacques Marquette, and René-Robert Cavelier de La Salle, surveyed much of the great river, reaching its mouth in 1682. Then, in 1699, King Louis XIV, upon learning that the English were about to send ships to set up a colony along the Mississippi coast, dispatched Pierre d'Iberville to the region. D'Iberville beat the English to the prize, founding a French settlement at Biloxi Bay, the first permanent European outpost in the region. Over the next two decades, other French settlements followed: at Mobile, also on the Gulf Coast, Fort Rosalie near Natchez, and New Orleans in 1718. The settlers named this new province Louisiana, in honor of their king, and quickly set about trying to win over the local Indians, particularly the Choctaw, Chickasaw, and Natchez.

Despite these early efforts by Spain and France to colonize the Southeast, in the end it was the British who succeeded in dominating the region—and the native peoples who lived there. Although Britain's first attempt to establish a colony on Roanoke Island off the coast of North Carolina failed dismally in the 1580s, its second attempt at Jamestown in nearby Virginia in 1607 took root and prospered.

Yet it was not Jamestown, but Charles Towne, established farther south in the Carolina Territory, that had the greatest impact on the southeastern Indians. Founded in 1670 by a band of British merchants, Charles

French explorer La Salle, standing sword in hand next to a crude cross, claims the Mississippi Valley for King Louis XIV in April 1682, as groups of local Indians look on. La Salle's claim created the vast Louisiana Territory, bought 121 years later by the fledgling United States.

Towne quickly developed into a booming port of trade. The Indians living in the vicinity of the settlement suddenly found themselves inundated with offers by British traders to exchange a variety of European manufactured goods, from guns to metal pots and blankets, for two important commodities: deerskins, a source of leather in Europe at the time; and Indian captives, who were sold to work as slaves on plantations in Carolina, New England, and the West Indies.

Of all the goods introduced from Europe, one in particular—alcohol—proved especially destructive. Although the Indians likened it to a "poisonous plant" and assigned their healers the task of finding an antidote to its sickness, many could not resist its mood-altering properties. "Most of the [Catawbas] are much addicted to drunkenness, a vice they never were acquainted with, till the Christians came amongst them," noted John Lawson in his journal in 1701. "Some of them refrain drinking strong liquors, but very few of that sort are found among them. Their chief liquor is rum, without any mixture. This the English bring among them, and buy skins, furs, slaves, and other of their commodities therewith." Drunkenness, often encouraged by unscrupulous traders who saw it as a way of gaining an advantage over the Indians, became a serious health hazard in many communities. "In drunken frolics (which are always carried on in the night)," wrote Lawson, "they sometimes murder one another, fall into the fire, fall down precipices, and break their necks, with several other misfortunes which this drinking of rum brings upon them; and though they are sensible of it, yet they have no power to refrain this enemy." Some Indian leaders opposed the sale of rum to their people and tried to ban it from their towns; but they eventually gave up such efforts, mostly because of protests from their own young men.

By the year 1699, trade between the Carolina colonists and southeastern Indians had grown to such an extent that Charles Towne merchants were exporting perhaps 54,000 deerskins annually to Europe. In 1707 more than 121,000 marketable pelts left Charles Towne harbor, and in the decades that followed, the annual take was often double this figure. This massive slaughter was in many ways a prelude to the massacre of the buffalo on the Great Plains a century and a half later. It changed forever the nature of hunting in the Southeast. Indians who once stalked deer solely to feed and clothe their families now became commercial hunters, armed more often with guns than bows and arrows and seeking an ever increasing bounty of hides. Many tribes exhausted the supply of deer in their own territory and were forced to roam far afield in pursuit of game. The competition for hunting grounds grew fierce, leading to increased intertribal rivalry and eventually to full-scale wars.

But nothing caused the Indians to fight among themselves as much as the insatiable demand for slaves. In their initial bartering sessions with Carolina traders, the Indians found they could get good prices for captives they had taken in war. So as soon as they had traded away all their existing prisoners, they sought to acquire more. Thus the purpose of tribal warfare switched from settling blood feuds to procuring captives to sell to the white men. The Chickasaw became particularly notorious in their quest for slaves, attacking weaker tribes with ruthless efficiency. At first the Chickasaw raided only nearby tribes, such as the Choctaw and the Yazoo. Soon, however, encouraged and armed by Carolina merchants, they extended their forays farther north and west across the Mississippi, where they ravaged the Caddo and other tribes residing along the lower Arkansas and Red Rivers.

Pitting one tribe against another was a strategy used by all three European powers as they vied for financial and imperial gain. Carolina's Englishmen were especially proficient at sowing war, arming the Yamasee against the Guale and the Timucua from 1680 to 1690; the Yamasee and Muskogee against the Apalachee from 1702 to 1704; and the Yamasee, Chickasaw, and Muskogee against the Choctaw from 1690 to 1710. Several Florida tribes—the Apalachee, Calusa, and Timucua—paid perhaps the heaviest price in these ruthless land and trade wars. In 1704, hoping to extinguish any remaining Spanish influence in the Southeast, the Carolinians dispatched a combined force of 50 English soldiers and 1,000 Creek and other warriors to western Florida. There they attacked a string of Spanish missions, killing or enslaving thousands of Calusa, Timucua, and Apalachee Indians. These Florida tribes were easy prey for the English and Creeks because Spanish policy prohibited them from owning guns. After the slaughter, only tiny remnants of these once populous and prosperous peoples remained. Most survivors fled to Cuba or other Spanish-held islands in the West Indies.

Over the course of the next few years, English-led bands of Chickasaws, frequently supported by Creeks, assaulted Choctaw settlements in the French-controlled lands east of the Mississippi River, destroying many towns and taking a significant number of prisoners. The French sought repeatedly to make peace between the two tribes. But the Chickasaw appetite for English goods, which were more plentiful and of higher quality than those of the French, combined with their ancient enmity for the

Traces of paint cling to a small hardwood figure of a medicine man, carved by an artisan of the Caddoan group in the lower Mississippi Valley. Furnished with a mustache and a wig of human hair, the figure grasps a cloth bundle containing sacred amulets.

Choctaw, kept the two rivals almost constantly at each other's throats.

By the first decade of the 18th century, only the strongest tribes of the region remained, all of the smaller groups having been either exterminated or absorbed. Some of the Carolina colonists feared that the policy of promoting strife among the Indians, coupled with the growing mistreatment of them, might backfire and spark a pan-Indian rebellion. A few voices even began to speak out, among them the explorer John Lawson. He observed in his journal that native peoples were "really better to us than we have been to them. They always give us victuals at their quarters," he noted, "and take care we are armed against hunger and thirst: We do not do so by them, but let them walk by our doors hungry and do not often relieve them. We look upon them with scorn and disdain, and think them little better than beasts in human shape."

In 1707 a group of English reformists persuaded the Carolina Assembly to pass an Indian trade act that created a board of commissioners to issue licenses to traders. The act also established the post of Indian agent, whose job it was to travel among the tribes for 10 months of every year, listening to complaints against traders and meting out punishments. The first man chosen to fill this post was Thomas Nairne, an outspoken Carolina planter-politician. Almost immediately upon taking the job, Nairne arrested a trader, James Child, on charges of Indian abuse. Nairne specifically accused Child of illegally leading a group of Cherokees on a slaving raid against another tribe friendly to the British. The raid had netted Child 160 Indian captives, all of whom he sold into slavery at a hefty profit.

Many colonists, however, did not approve of Child's arrest, nor did they want the Indian trade reformed. After Nairne returned from a lengthy inspection of Creek and Chickasaw lands, he was arrested on trumped-up charges of treason. Although he was eventually freed, he lost his job and never served as Indian agent again.

Nairne's successors did not share his zeal for reform. Traders continued to set Indian against Indian, and to mistreat even their most loyal Indian allies. When the Yamasee, who had faithfully fought numerous wars on behalf of the English, could not provide the Carolina traders with enough captives, the traders began snatching the Yamasee themselves and selling them into bondage. The outrage drove the Yamasee from the English camp. With the cooperation of other angry tribes, they began plotting revenge. Ironically, among the first white casualties were two men who had at least made some effort to speak on the Indians' behalf—John Lawson and Thomas Nairne.

THE SEMINOLE MEDICINE MAN

In the traditional Seminole world, ordinary events are imbued with extraordinary causes and meanings. Everyday items are believed to have uncommon powers. The shadow world is populated by agents—animals, ghosts, witches, and powers—who bring to the people illness and pain, insight, love, and delight. The medicine man possesses the knowledge and the power to deal with such forces.

The medicine man is the Seminole community's religious leader, charged with learning, preserving, and teaching essential beliefs about the people's relationships with each other as well as with the natural and unearthly world. He is the tribe's political adviser, responsible for keeping group decisions and policies in harmony with unseen powers. And he is the family doctor, expected to restore health when injury or illness strikes.

The beliefs, methods, and ceremonies of the medicine men of the Five Civilized Tribes sprang from common roots in a culture that was once closely shared. To a remarkable degree, the Seminoles of Oklahoma have preserved the old ways in spite of the wrenching events that uprooted and displaced the tribe. One of their number, Willie Lena of Wewoka, observed the traditions of the medicine men practically from his birth in 1912, and later recorded them in artful drawings. His knowledge provides a rare glimpse of an unseen world.

A Seminole healer's medicine bag—a buckskin pouch with a protective cover and shoulder strap—contains his most often used herbal remedies, wound dressings, implements, and sacred objects.

A traditional Seminole medicine man, sketched by Willie Lena, carries in his right hand his badge of office—the bubbling stick. The feather he wears, from an owl, signifies that he has multiple healing specialties. A buzzard feather would denote expertise in treating wounds; a yellow flicker feather identifies a headache specialist.

A rattle made from a box turtle shell—crafted, decorated, and blessed by a conjurer—is used in Seminole ceremonies and dances.

A medicine man harvesting herbal remedies stuffs them in this bundle, which is strapped to his wrist to keep both of his hands free for gathering.

THE CURATIVE POWER OF PLANTS

"A Seminole doctor doesn't treat just anyone," Willie Lena related. A preliminary interview is conducted to determine whether the patient believes in traditional medicine and whether he can pay for treatment—not to enrich the healer, but to ensure results.

If the patient is acceptable, the medicine man diagnoses the complaint. Usually he detects the ill will of a particular animal spirit, which can be placated with a dose of a certain herbal remedy. Kidney stones, for example, are attributed to some offense against the rabbit spirit and are treated with "rabbit medicine," a tea made from milkweed.

To be effective, the medicine must be not only correctly identified but also properly gathered, prepared, and administered. The accurate rendition of the appropriate curing songs at each step is believed to be as essential as the medicine itself. Also crucial is the medicine man's follow-up advice, which in the case of kidney stones prohibits greasy food and heavy lifting.

A medicine man gathering beneficial plants holds two stalks of button snakeroot, which he will steep to make "pasa," a medicinal tea and purgative. He regards a stand of small pussy willows, whose roots he will bruise and steep to make "hoyvnijv," which contains an ingredient of aspirin.

The Seminole conjurer's equipment includes the medicine pot (left) for steeping herbal decoctions and the bubbling stick (below) to blow into and mix the brew.

Before he takes some roots of a tree for medicine, a Seminole healer first walks four times around the tree, praying to its spirit. He crouches, arms dangling, in order to receive the power of the tree.

A medicine man blows through his bubbling stick into a pot of herbs steeping in water. He is stirring the mixture while adding to it the power of his breath and his healing incantations.

A HEALER'S DIVERSE TOOLS

A medicine man (above) lures a legendary Giant Horned Snake from its watery lair with fresh sumac twigs and rituals. Scrapings said to be taken from the snake's horn are regarded as an especially potent medicine.

In addition to scores of plants, the Seminole pharmacopoeia includes potions made from parts of animals, birds, and insects. Ever since a tribesman ill with tuberculosis improved after accidentally being sprayed in the face by a skunk, the animal's potent scent, much diluted, has been used to treat the disease. The origins of other remedies—boiled pigs' knuckles for whooping cough, for example, or dried animal bone marrow for coagulating the blood of a wound—are lost to memory.

Other standard procedures include ritual scratching and bloodletting in a manner that resembles, but predates, similar early European practice. The use of a miniature bow and arrow to lance boils and sties requires, especially in the latter case, considerable skill to avoid doing the patient more harm than good.

A healer feeds his "sapiya," colored stones whose powerful magic can turn against their owner unless they are nurtured with squirrel blood and dew.

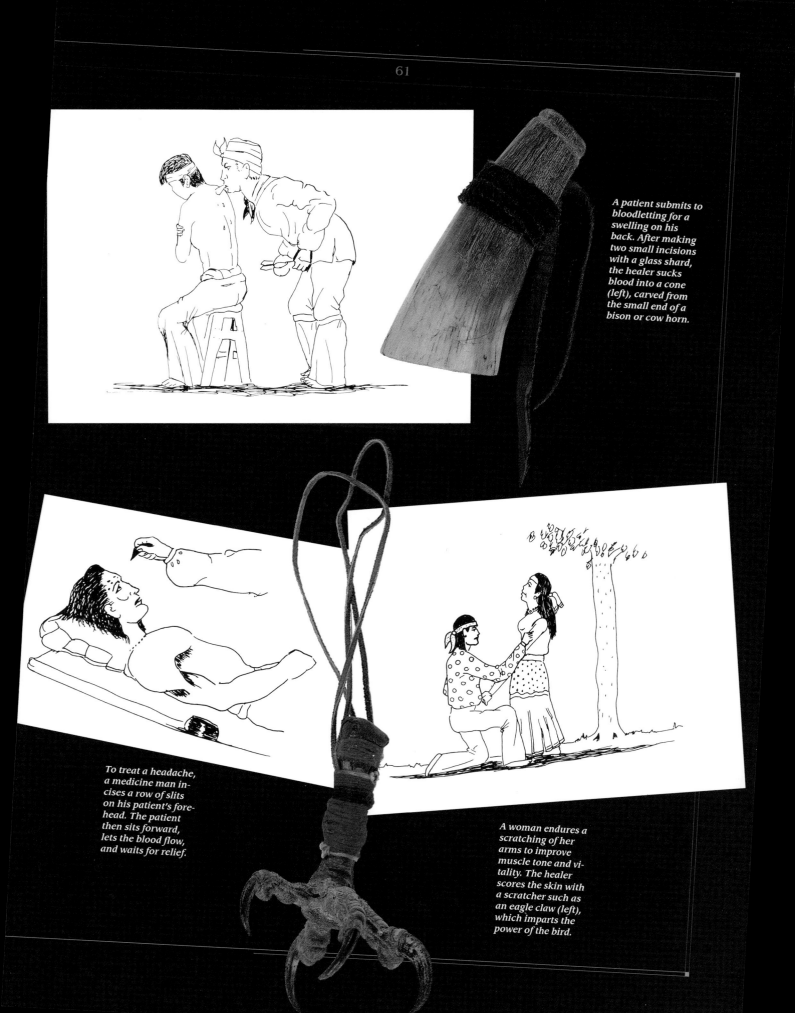

A patient submits to bloodletting for a swelling on his back. After making two small incisions with a glass shard, the healer sucks blood into a cone (left), carved from the small end of a bison or cow horn.

To treat a headache, a medicine man incises a row of slits on his patient's forehead. The patient then sits forward, lets the blood flow, and waits for relief.

A woman endures a scratching of her arms to improve muscle tone and vitality. The healer scores the skin with a scratcher such as an eagle claw (left), which imparts the power of the bird.

FIGHTING MALEVOLENT FORCES

A medicine man is expected to deal not only with illness but also with the forces of nature and malevolent powers, whether they be human or unearthly. Foiling witches is a special and constant concern. These evil humans are said to assume the forms of animals or birds, often that of the great horned owl, in pursuit of innocent victims whom they afflict with sickness and bad luck.

A medicine man can use an owl's talon to remove a witch's spell from the body of its victim. In order to safeguard a house, he fixes an owl's feather over the front door. Spells can be lifted from food or drink by the use of a precautionary cleansing formula, and from inside a house with the smoke of cedar leaves. If all else fails, a witch can be killed, but only with a special arrow that has been fletched with owl feathers.

A medicine man strives to divert an approaching tornado. If his pleas, intensified by the eagle-feathered prayer stick planted at his feet, should fail, he relies on the specially prepared terrapin shell (above, right) mounted on the stick before him to disable the twister.

A medicine man, accompanied by a relative of a murder victim, ceremonially smokes his pipe while burning a clay effigy of the unknown killer. If the figure falls over in the flames, the murderer is expected to die within four days.

To prevent witches from entering a house and leaving bad medicine, the prudent Seminole hangs an owl feather (right) over the entrance. Smoke from cedar leaves (left) is believed to cleanse the home of evil intentions.

After ritually sweeping the dance ground prior to the Green Corn Ceremony, a medicine man carefully places twigs from his broom in the post of an arbor. This "killing of the green wood" neutralizes harmful magic.

The designated "feather whooper" uses a wand like this one to notify the birds that the Feather Dance in their honor—part of the Green Corn Ceremony's third day—is about to commence.

A medicine man (left) prays over the purified site of the new fire that will light the Green Corn Ceremony's sacred rituals. He must arrange four logs, and alongside them four sacrificial ears of corn, in the correct sequence and position in order to ensure success.

Leaning on buffalo canes, shaking their heads from side to side, bellowing, and stamping, Seminole dancers imitate bison in the dramatic Buffalo Dance, which provides a climax for the Green Corn Ceremony's eventful third day.

A Seminole matron, her finest traditional costume bedecked with ribbons, begins the women's Ribbon Dance, the principal event of the Green Corn Ceremony's second day. She carries a knife-shaped wooden club (below, right) to denote her role as dance leader.

A PURIFYING SUMMER CEREMONY

From early spring to late fall, the Seminole year is punctuated by ceremonies designed to foster the well-being of the community. Conducted in a square ground—actually a square within a circle 40 yards in diameter—the most important of these rituals is the Green Corn Ceremony, or Busk, held in June or July. The medicine man plays an integral role in these proceedings.

The ceremony begins with the cleansing and renewal of the square ground, the center of Seminole religious life, and the lighting of the sacred fire. There follows a sequence of rites, dancing, and feasting. These activities are designed to purify the men of the village so they can eat the ripening corn; initiate youngsters into the community; propitiate important animal spirits; reaffirm the community's fealty to its chief and medicine man; and invoke prosperity and happiness for all the people.

The Three Cherokees, came over from the head of the River Savanna to London 1762
& their Interpreter that was Poisoned.

THE RAVAGES OF WARFARE

Three Cherokee leaders appear with an English interpreter in an engraving based on a 1762 drawing. The Indians were sent to London by the governor of Virginia as a goodwill gesture to the powerful tribe. They would have carried pipes, such as the one above, for social and ritual smoking.

Early in April of 1715, two exhausted and shaken traders hurried into Charles Towne. They had been riding almost nonstop for several days and brought hair-raising news. The Lower Creeks, with the backing of the Apalachee and Yamasee, were plotting to kill all of the Carolina traders, destroy their trading posts, and swoop down on the widely scattered and vulnerable plantations. A friendly Yamasee had divulged the secret to the Indian wife of one of the traders while he was off hunting runaway slaves in northeastern Florida. The southeastern Indians' smoldering resentment of the exploitive Carolina trading system was about to burst into flame, touching off a conflagration that would shatter the existing order in the South.

Carolina governor Charles Craven acted with dispatch. Scarcely allowing the two traders time to catch their breath, he ordered them to Pocotaligo, one of the Yamasee towns in the area around Port Royal, south of Charles Towne, with a peace delegation of officials that included Thomas Nairne, the respected former Indian agent. Craven instructed his representatives to give the Indians assurances that all their grievances would be redressed at an upcoming conference.

Craven had good reason to turn first to the Yamasee. Their towns screened Carolina's southern flank from possible Spanish attacks, and the colonists considered them among their staunchest allies. In 1712 the Yamasee had played a major role in helping their English trading partners defeat the Tuscarora in North Carolina.

The longstanding English indifference to the rights of the Indians had triggered that conflict. It erupted after a band of Tuscaroras captured John Lawson, who had become surveyor general of North Carolina, and condemned him to death. Without so much as a nod to the Tuscarora, Lawson arranged the sale of 17,500 acres of their land between the Neuse and Trent Rivers to a Swiss baron named Christoph von Graffenried, for the establishment of the town of New Bern as a haven for Swiss and German Protestants escaping Catholic persecution in Europe.

After years of seeing their sons and daughters corrupted with rum, swindled, debauched, sold into slavery, and killed defending their families, the Tuscarora were a people at bay. Lawson's land sale was the last straw. In 1710 the tribe had even offered to relinquish their homes in North Carolina in exchange for a more peaceful site in Pennsylvania. But the Pennsylvania colonial officials rejected the plea, claiming that before negotiations could take place, the tribe would have to procure a certificate of good behavior from Carolina authorities that would "confirm the sincerity of their past carriage toward the English." The Tuscarora refused this humiliating demand and bided their time until they made Lawson the first victim of their wrath at the Tuscarora town of Catechna in September 1711. Before the Tuscarora were overwhelmed by the Carolinians and their Indian allies, they killed several hundred colonists and nearly succeeded in destroying New Bern. After shipping a portion of the tribe off into slavery, the Carolinians permitted the majority of Tuscaroras to emigrate to upper New York State, where they were taken in by the Oneida Indians and eventually became the sixth nation in the Iroquois League.

Now, in 1715, the English in South Carolina faced the specter of another such catastrophe. Governor Craven hoped that his delegates to the Yamasee would keep the peace, but in fact a new conflict erupted that would prove even more costly for everyone concerned.

The Carolinians arrived at Pocotaligo on April 14. Matters seemed to go well at first. Yamasee headmen received the colonial representatives politely, and the two groups partook of the ritual black drink. That night, however, while the English visitors slept, Yamasee warriors put on their red and black war paint. At dawn they surprised the Carolinians in their tents, killing several outright. The others, among them Thomas Nairne, were ritually tortured to death.

In the weeks that followed, the Indians fell upon the Port Royal planters, killing whomever they could lay hands on, slaughtering livestock, and torching farms. Several hundred settlers saved themselves by crowding onto a ship that lay at anchor beyond the range of the Indians' weapons. Soon colonists all across South Carolina were abandoning their farms and streaming into Charles Towne.

Governor Craven mobilized the Carolina militia and counterattacked. Marching at the head of 250 militiamen and settlement Indians, the governor drove off a number of Yamasees camped near the headwaters of the Combahee River in late April. Meanwhile, other militiamen stormed Pocotaligo and captured a vast store of supplies. The loss of their towns caused the Yamasee to pull back to safety south of the Savannah River.

Tuscarora Indians dance around poles covered with wolf skins during execution rites in September 1711 for John Lawson, Baron Christoph von Graffenried, and the latter's black servant. The Indians spared the black man and Graffenried, who later drew this sketch of his brush with death.

The flames of conflict, however, had spread far and wide. By now the Indians of coastal Carolina were in full-scale revolt. Excepting the faraway Chickasaw and most of the Cherokee towns, practically every Indian community from the Florida border to Cape Fear, North Carolina, was at war, with the Lower Creeks leading the revolt. From his parish in Goose Creek, northwest of Charles Towne, Francis Le Jau, an Anglican minister, ominously reported that the Indians "surround us on every side but the sea."

The Carolina Assembly hastily granted Governor Craven emergency powers to bolster the militia's thin ranks with black slaves and to dispatch agents to solicit guns, ammunition, and more troops from New England and Virginia. As the summer wore on and reinforcements and supplies began arriving on the Charles Towne docks, the Indians scaled back their attacks. But small war parties continued to strike unwary colonists, preventing a return to normal life. "They carry all their estates about with them, and are never far from home or out of their way," one frustrated Englishman said of the warriors. "A little parched corn and puddle water is good victuals for them and fattens them like hogs."

With the harvest season coming on, Carolina's fate rested with the powerful Cherokee. Living far inland in the vastness of the Appalachian high country, the Cherokee had not suffered as many abuses at the hands of the Carolinians as had the coastal tribes, and subsequently they had not murdered their traders—although a few towns had allowed their warriors to fight alongside the Catawba. Moreover, enmity between the Cherokee and the Creek nations was longstanding. If the bulk of the Cherokees could be persuaded to remain neutral, Craven reasoned—or better yet, to ally with the Carolinians—the colony would be saved.

Two traders, Eleazer Wigan and Robert Gilcrest, agreed to travel to Cherokee country to negotiate an alliance. They went first to the town of Echota, located along the headwaters of the Chattahoochee River. The traders managed to win over the town council, and in October, a delegation led by a war leader called Caesar by the English traveled to Charles Towne to conclude an accord.

Mistakenly assuming that the Echota ambassadors represented the entire Cherokee Nation, the English planned a joint military operation designed to crush the rebellious Creeks and end the war. While a combined Cherokee-English force sacked the Upper Creek towns, the main body of Carolinians would attack the Lower Creeks and their allies. But when it came time for the Cherokees to link up with the English, they failed to appear. Craven sent Colonel Maurice Moore and a force of 300 black and white troops to the Cherokee town of Tugaloo to resolve the issue.

On December 29, 1715, the Tugaloo Cherokees welcomed the Carolinians with ceremonial eagle wings and ushered them into their council house to be received by Charitey Hagey, their influential headman, known as The Conjurer by the English. Intent on preventing a wider war, Hagey and his supporters had persuaded the majority of the lower Cherokee towns to maintain a position of neutrality. The Cherokees, he informed Moore, were prepared to support the English on certain conditions. They would fight against some of the tribes, such as the Apalachee, but not against the Yamasee, whom Charitey Hagey called "his ancient people." Most encouraging of all to the Carolinians, he informed Moore that he had already sent a flag of truce to the Upper Creeks, and that a party of their headmen was on its way to Tugaloo to discuss a resolution to the crisis.

Again the Carolinians assumed that a single Indian leader had the authority to speak for all of the people. In fact Charitey Hagey represented only one Cherokee faction. Even as he was promising peace, a pro-English faction led by Caesar, eager to gain captives for trading purposes, was planning to attack the Creeks. Meanwhile, an anti-English faction was plotting to ally with the Creeks and massacre Moore and his men.

In late January, the Creek delegation arrived. During a secret meeting held in the council house, the Creek leaders attempted to persuade the Cherokees to turn on the British. As the Creeks argued, several hundred of their warriors waited in the forest outside Tugaloo. What followed was one of the most dramatic events in the 300-year conflict between whites and Indians in North America.

No one will ever know exactly how it happened—many Carolinians would later ascribe it to Divine Providence—but suddenly, without any warning, the winter's calm was broken by the cries of war. Caesar and his followers attacked the Creek delegates and put every one of them to the knife. The stunning *coup de main* shattered the southeastern Indian custom of ensuring the safety of emissaries and, at a stroke, plunged the entire Cherokee Nation into war. The Cherokees then joined with Moore in driving the Creek forces from the surrounding woods, hounding the retreating warriors until none was left to track.

The dramatic events at Tugaloo effectively ended the Yamasee War. Caught between the Carolinians on the coast and the mighty Cherokee in the west, the Catawba and other tribes of the Carolina Piedmont sued for peace. The angry Creeks held out until 1717, when they finally accepted a shaky truce. But they would be slow to forgive the Cherokee treachery, and bad blood between the two nations would continue for decades.

This suited the Carolinians. The Yamasee War had cost them 400 dead and nearly destroyed their economy. Although the ruined crops could easily be replanted and the stocks of cattle and pigs replenished, rebuilding the lucrative deerskin trade was another matter. A first step was to enact more stringent trading standards to prevent future abuses of the Indians. Henceforth, traders would have to post bond in the colony of their legal residence before they could operate in specific Indian towns. If a trader failed to abide by the new regulations, he forfeited his bond.

In the meantime, the British authorities began taking political steps to prevent the rise of any future tribal confederacies that might threaten their trading empire. In essence the English determined to follow the old rule of

divide and conquer. They would foment discord among the tribes by pitting Indian against Indian. In particular the Carolinians vowed to sustain the Creek-Cherokee feud. "This makes the matter of great weight to us," explained one colonist, "how to hold both as our friends, and assist them in cutting one another's throats. This is the game we intend to play."

The Yamasee War transformed the map of the Southeast. Ravaged by disease as well as warfare, the small coastal tribes withered. The Lower Creeks, who had moved east to the Ocmulgee River to be closer to their Carolinian trading partners, now abandoned their towns and withdrew westward to their old homeland along the Chattahoochee River. While a few Yamasees sought refuge with Creeks and Catawbas, the bulk of the tribe fled to Florida.

But whether the Indians were forced to move or not, in the aftermath of the Yamasee War it became clear that the southeastern peoples had also lost something more important—their economic independence. Although trade with the whites had long since become a necessity, the war showed, as never before, that the Indians had become trapped in a deadly economic web. In the decades that followed, hostilities in the region would multiply as competition for trading advantages intensified. Thus began a century-long contest that the Indians would find ultimately unwinnable—the struggle to ensure a steady supply of European trade goods and technology without forfeiting their freedom of action.

Ironically, the Creek, not the Cherokee, were best positioned to play this game. By siding with the English in the Yamasee War, the Cherokee had cut themselves off from developing commercial links to the French and Spaniards and consequently grew ever more dependent on the English. Hostile Creeks would not allow Cherokees through their territory to Florida, and the Choctaw blocked their path to Louisiana. The Creek, on the other hand, were advantageously situated. Ensconced in what is today Alabama and Georgia, they had access on three sides to the European powers—Spain in the south, France in the west, and Britain in the east. And for most of the 18th century, they turned this coincidence of geography to advantage by playing one European nation against another.

The miko of the Lower Creek town of Coweta, called Emperor Brims by the English, increased his influence by playing a consummate diplomatic hand. Brims encouraged the Spaniards to build a fort at Coweta, yet also welcomed the construction of a French stronghold, Fort Toulouse, at the junction of the Coosa and Tallapoosa Rivers—one of the most valuable strategic positions in the South. When British emissaries came to discuss an accord with the people of Coweta, Brims gave his niece in marriage to the son of a leading member of the British delegation. Shortly afterward, when this same English emissary returned from Charles Towne to seal a treaty, Brims had to be summoned

The pieces of clothing shown here belonged to Seminole leader Hillis Hadjo, known to English colonists as Francis. They include a shirt, leggings, and moccasins of smoke-cured buckskin, along with a hand-woven wool bag.

A Choctaw man demonstrates the art of shooting a cane blowgun, a weapon used by southeastern Indians to kill small game. Feathered with thistledown, wooden darts like the ones shown here could be projected as far as 25 yards.

from a meeting with a Creek delegation that had recently returned from visiting Spanish officials in Mexico City. "No one has ever been able to make him take sides with one of the three European nations," commented one French official. Partly because of the diplomacy of Brims and his successors, the Creek were able to retain their position of strength for several generations—even as they maintained their blood feud with the Cherokee.

Farther west, the competition for trade exacerbated the traditional enmity between the Chickasaw and the Choctaw. The Chickasaw had always been staunch allies of the British, who kept them well supplied with trade goods, often in exchange for Choctaw captives. Chickasaw women used British hoes to turn the earth and British textiles to make clothing for their families, while their husbands owned British guns, knives, and hatchets. Meanwhile, a number of British traders had taken Chickasaw wives and were raising families. All these changes cemented Chickasaw loyalty to Great Britain.

The Choctaw supported the French, who had sup-

European trade goods had become a part of Indian life when the Georgia settler Philip von Reck made these sketches in the early 1700s. The hunters below, one carrying a musket, wear a mixture of white and Indian garb. In the Creek hunting camp at bottom, an imported kettle hangs beside a deerskin.

plied them with guns for self-defense when the tribe was being ravaged by Chickasaw and Creek slave raids. But the French connection had strings attached that many Choctaws found unacceptable. As a result, several towns entered the British trade orbit, either by traveling to Chickasaw towns to buy and sell or by welcoming Carolina traders into their midst.

Beginning about 1720, England and France began competing for the allegiance of each other's trading partners. First the French tried to lure the Chickasaw away from the English by alternately offering gifts and threatening war. When these ventures failed, the French encouraged their Choctaw allies to attack English traders entering Chickasaw country. Provoked, the Chickasaw raided Choctaw towns and attacked French settlements and supply boats. So effective were the Chickasaw that the French were forced to halt nearly all trade and communications along the lower Mississippi River for several years.

Calm returned to the Mississippi in 1725. But it was merely the lull before another storm. Now the English took the initiative, using their Chickasaw friends to woo local tribes away from the French. The chief result of this effort in Indian diplomacy was to destroy the Natchez Indians living along the lower Mississippi River. Beleaguered by French settlers, the Natchez welcomed the Chickasaw overtures. Emboldened by promises of

English support, the Natchez attacked Fort Rosalie, killing some 250 Frenchmen and taking 300 women and children prisoner. In all likelihood, the Natchez considered the victory a just reprisal for their own losses in the years past. But their thirst for revenge would cost them dearly. By 1731 the French and their Choctaw allies had virtually annihilated the tribe. Those few Natchez who escaped death or enslavement sought refuge among the Chickasaw, Creek, and Cherokee. The Natchez War expanded hostilities in the Southeast. Throughout the 1730s, the French, aided by the Choctaw, staged numerous attacks on Chickasaw settlements. But time and again, the Chickasaw managed to repulse their European foe.

The strain of constant warfare took a heavy toll on all the Indians living in the western part of the region. But the Choctaw suffered especially, and by the 1740s, the three traditional divisions of the tribe had hardened into hostile factions. While the eastern towns maintained their historic friendship with the French, the western towns began looking to the English for trade and protection. A cluster of towns to the south, meanwhile, divided their loyalties between the two European nations. The discord exploded into civil war in the late 1740s. For two years, the Choctaws killed each other. More than 800 warriors from the western towns died—including their war leader, Red Shoe. The fighting so demoralized the tribe that it agreed to a harsh treaty dictated by the French. Under its terms, any Choctaw who even entertained an English visitor would be executed. The accord also stipulated that the tribe maintain its enmity toward the Chickasaw, continuing "to strike at that perfidious race as long as there should be any portion of it remaining."

The years of bloodshed hastened the process of cultural change. Unable to cultivate their fields properly because of the fighting, the Choctaw could no longer produce sufficient harvests. Under the pressure of hunger, their political and social institutions were fraying. Previously, decisions affecting the tribe had been arrived at by consensus in open council meetings. Now factions with interests tied to either the French or the English were likely to make their own plans, disregarding town consensus.

In the 1750s, France and England began their final battle for hegemony in the New World. Indians in the eastern third of the continent were soon dragged into the fighting on the side of their respective trading partners. For the Cherokee, the French and Indian War, as the conflict came to be known in American history, would prove particularly destructive.

Choctaw women stand by the doorway of a traditional thatched house fashioned of palmetto fronds overlaying a frame of logs in a photograph taken near Lake Pontchartrain in southern Louisiana about the year 1880.

At first the entire Cherokee Nation supported the British. When Iroquois and Choctaw allies of the French attacked their towns, the Cherokee appealed to their trading partners to establish garrisons in their territory, and the British complied. The Cherokee then agreed to send warriors to help the British campaign against the French and Shawnee in the Ohio River valley. During a bitter winter, a Cherokee war party set off for the valley, making their way through storms and heavy snow. Finally, having lost both horses and provisions to the elements, they were forced to turn back. Near the Virginia border, the hungry warriors encountered a few cows wandering in the woods. The Indians, desperate for food, slaughtered the animals and ate them. When the white owners discovered their loss, they went after the Cherokees and killed and scalped several of them.

Determined to avenge the outrage, the clansmen of the dead warriors embarked on a series of raids against English settlements. Meanwhile, tribal elders sought to iron out the disagreement, trying to find a means to balance the legitimate demand for revenge by the families of the murdered men with the larger tribal need for good relations with the English. First the Indians sent a delegation to Charles Towne to arrange a truce. Then a large body of headmen—32 in all—agreed to assemble at Fort Prince George, a British stronghold in South Carolina, to work out an agreement. The entire endeavor misfired. South Carolina's governor ignored the peacemaking nature of the visit and imprisoned the Cherokee representatives, demanding the tribe turn in all those responsible for the raids. The Cherokee offered a few concessions, and the governor released three of the men, among them a war chief named Oconostota. As soon as he was freed, Oconostota gathered his forces, laid siege to the fort, and demanded a conference with the commander. When the officer in charge

stepped from behind the stockade, Oconostota gave the signal to attack. At this, British soldiers murdered the remainder of the Cherokee peace party still in their hands.

The incident triggered a fresh burst of Cherokee attacks along the Carolina frontier. The Cherokees also besieged a British fort in Tennessee. Determined to bring the Indians under their control, the British launched two major campaigns. In the first, in June 1760, British troops destroyed all the lower Cherokee towns along the banks of the Savannah River. Many Indians were killed, and the remainder were forced into the mountains. The British returned the next summer with a larger force, including Chickasaw and Choctaw warriors. The Anglo-Indian army proceeded to sack the middle Cherokee towns. A lieutenant cataloged the scene on one particularly destructive day. "We proceeded by orders to burn the Indian cabins," he wrote in his journal. "Some of the men seemed to enjoy this cruel work, laughing heartily at the flames, but to me it appeared a shocking sight. When we came to cut down the fields of corn, I could scarcely refrain from tears. Who, without grief, could see the stately stalks with broad green leaves and tasseled shocks, the staff of life, sink under our swords with all their precious load?" With no corn to sustain them, the Cherokee faced starvation. In weakened health, the tribe was vulnerable to a smallpox epidemic that took an unusually heavy toll. Perhaps half the entire Cherokee Nation died from the combined effects of war, famine, and disease.

British colonial officials make their annual presentation of gifts to their Indian trading partners in this 1838 engraving made from an early-18th-century drawing. To the southeastern Indians, gift giving represented tangible proof of friendship.

Despite their losses, the Cherokee—as well as other tribes who fought with the French against the British—remained a force to be reckoned with. Consequently, when Britain triumphed, gaining control of the continent, King George III attempted to ensure peace with the native peoples. The southeastern tribes, like other Indians living on the frontier, had long been troubled by a steady stream of colonists pouring westward into their hunting grounds. In a major policy statement designed to make North America more secure and governable, the king forbade all white settlement west of the Appalachians. He also ordered those settlers living beyond this boundary to abandon their homesteads and return east. The edict was largely ignored, however, and settlers headed west in ever greater numbers.

To make matters worse, the Indians were once again running up huge debts to the traders. In the four decades between the Yamasee War and the French and Indian War, something of a balance had been maintained. The French had lavished gifts on their Indian friends, offering free goods worth many thousands of deerskins. As one French official had noted, "All the chiefs of the Indians, even those remote from these posts, ordinarily go to the forest with the expectation of receiving some presents. That is what keeps them on our side." The British had no choice but to offer gifts as well. In addition, competition with the French had kept the cost of British goods low and encouraged fair trading practices.

With the French out of the picture, however, British traders once again resorted to unethical tactics. A common strategy was to ply the Indians with rum before making a deal. It was the custom for traders to greet hunters upon their return from the forest and offer them liquor, then demand skins in payment. Along the frontier, traders established saloons where Indians regularly drank themselves into insensitivity. After a few days of heavy alcohol consumption, the hunters would leave empty handed. As one observer noted, the merchants took the "fruit of three or four months toil," leaving the Indians "without the means of buying the necessary clothing for themselves or their families."

A combination of frustration with debt and a shortage of deer contributed to intensified intertribal competition. In the mid-1760s, for example, Creeks instigated a war with Choctaws, hoping to prevent them from trading with the British and to protect disputed hunting grounds. Before long the conflict had taken on a life of its own, resulting in a vicious cycle of blood revenge. Eventually Cherokees and Chickasaws joined the conflict on the side of the Choctaws. So many Indians died that winter, hunting had to be curtailed, resulting in a loss of skins to trade.

Overwhelmed by warfare and debt, the southeastern Indians began to yield to British pressure to cede small portions of their land. Between 1763 and 1773, for example, Creek leaders met six times with British officials to discuss cessions. At five of these conferences, they agreed to sell land to pay off trading debts. As a matter of fact, the land was often already overhunted or picked clean by settlers' livestock. Nevertheless, the land-for-debt swap was a dangerous precedent, one that would haunt the Creek, as well as other tribes, in the years to come.

It was during this period of crisis that a new Indian nation emerged in Florida—the Seminole. The tribe evolved following the Yamasee War, when the Yamasee moved from Carolina back into the region. Gradually the Yamasee were joined by remnants of other tribes. Later in the century, a town of Lower Creeks moved onto the Florida peninsula, seeking better hunting grounds. This group settled on the rich Alachua plains, near present-day Gainesville, eventually mingling with the earlier arrivals. In time, Creeks from other upper and lower towns joined them, establishing their own settlements all across northern Florida. This emerging nation—the Seminole tribe—also provided safe haven for a sizable number of escaped black slaves. The name of the tribe is probably derived from the Muskogee word for "runaway"—*simanoli.*

Although deerskin was the staple of Indian trade, colonists also purchased other products from the Indians, including bear grease. Packaged in attractive jars like these, the grease was sold by English merchants as a luxury hair pomade in America and Europe.

By the latter half of the 18th century, the way of life of the southeastern tribes had changed considerably. Although the Indians retained many features of their culture, especially those aspects related to their spiritual lives, their material culture became drastically altered. War and famine had taken their toll, and disease continued to reduce populations, even though some Indians had by now built up immunities. With the decline in numbers came changes in town life. Indian homes tended to be smaller than before. Although some resembled the notched log cabins of white settlers, most were still constructed in the traditional manner. Instead of erecting palisades around them, the Indians sought protection in colonial-style stockades, built and garrisoned by their white trading partners. This arrangement had its drawbacks for the Indians. The strongholds provided

By the late 18th century, gilt-decorated leather trunks like this one were part of the colonial trader's inventory. Other items included rifled and smoothbore muskets, ammunition, blankets, cloth, fishhooks, paint, knives, locks, hinges, and rum.

Silver earbobs like the ones above became a favorite trade item among southeastern Indians in the mid-18th century. Crafted by colonial silversmiths, the earbobs supplanted indigenous ear ornaments of shell and copper.

security, but they were also a means by which the colonials could pressure the Indians into accepting their demands. In many towns, the center of community life shifted from the council house to the trading post.

The items of daily life were radically different from those of the past. Firearms, once a novelty, were now the mainstay of hunting and warfare. Small-bore long rifles, accurate at 200 yards, had begun to replace the clumsy flintlock trade guns, and many towns had a resident gunsmith to repair them. Increasingly, metal farm implements, axes, saws, scissors, combs, and even mirrors were considered essential commodities.

The majority of Indians no longer dressed like their ancestors. Wool and cotton matchcoats, ruffled shirts, and calico skirts mingled with indigenous clothing; European jewelry and ribbons became common forms of adornment. Cloth turbans, sometimes decorated with imported ostrich feathers, became common headgear. Even war paint was no longer extracted from local sources, but often imported from overseas. As the Indians grew increasingly more dependent on European goods, traditional skills and craftsmanship eroded.

Major sociological changes were also occurring. The men, for example, were now almost exclusively occupied in commercial hunting, aimed at procuring trade goods, rather than meat for their families. Agricultural practices were changing as well. Along with the traditional corn, beans, and squash, the Indians cultivated many European crops, including wheat, rice, and fruit trees. They also began raising domestic animals and thus began fencing their fields to protect their crops from grazing livestock. Some Indians even branded their cattle and drove them to market in white towns. Horses, called *itchu lako*—or "big deer"—by the Creek, had become numerous, and the trade in mounts was an important economic activity.

Many southeastern tribes became ethnic melting pots. Early in the century, warfare had scattered the coastal tribes, and refugees had made homes among groups farther west. The Creek and the Catawba, in particular, had become patchworks of cultures.

The imported finery that is worn by this mid-18th-century Cherokee headman reflects his high status. His traditional blanket made from silver-trimmed British cloth is worn over a European-style ruffled shirt.

Among the newcomers were runaway black slaves from white plantations. For many years, of course, all the tribes had included white traders in their midst. But now, more and more Indian women married traders, raising children who took their white father's surname. Many of these mixed-blood progeny—who enjoyed the same kinship identity as all other Creeks and understood European speech and ways better—supplanted traditional tribal leaders. It was no longer rare to see an Indian with blue eyes or red hair.

At the same time, these marriages put enormous stress on the matrilineal kinship system. Traditionally, Indian husbands took up residence with their wives' families but were responsible for the children of their sisters—their clan kin. Property remained within the clan regardless of marital ties. But in their marriages to Indian women, the white traders followed the European practice that made the nuclear family the focus—wives moved into the homes of their white husbands, and fathers raised their own offspring and typically passed along property to wife and children. It was not uncommon, for instance, for a son of mixed ancestry to take over a trading post from his white father. In time, the prospect of a connection to the white world, with its wealth and power, along with the promise of inherited property, made such marriages more acceptable to some elements of the Indian community.

In the 1770s, the Indians were forced to confront yet another challenge to their way of life—the fight for independence by the American colonies. Most southeastern communities would have preferred to stay out of the conflict. But while the British and the Americans both voiced their wishes for Indian neutrality, they were soon conniving to enlist allies. When forced to pick sides, most tribes chose the British, fearing that an American victory would unleash hordes of settlers, almost all of whom were supporters of the Revolution, in part because the Crown had kept them off Indian lands. The conflict was to be particularly catastrophic for the Cherokee, who had not yet recovered from losses suffered in the French and Indian War. In the summer of 1776, the tribe began a series of raids on frontier settlements

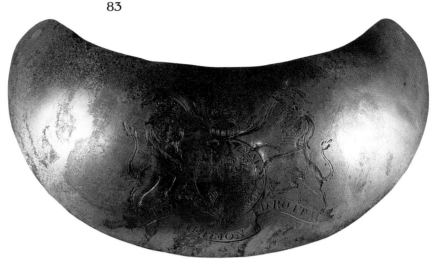

Found at a Chicka-saw site in northern Mississippi, this six-inch-long silver gor-get, like the one worn by the Chero-kee headman on the opposite page, bears a British coat of arms and a 1798 London hallmark.

from Virginia to Georgia. The raids were timed to coincide with the British assault on Charles Towne. Cherokee warriors, with British assistance, also attacked an American stockade in western South Carolina and in August ambushed and scattered a mounted militia force along the Seneca River.

In response the Americans unleashed a merciless scorched-earth campaign. First, they invaded lower Cherokee territory, destroying a number of towns and wiping out stores of food meant to carry the residents through the winter. But worse was yet to come. In early autumn, an army of troops from Virginia, North Carolina, and Georgia marched through the remainder of the Cherokee towns, destroying everything in their path. By the end of the campaign, some 50 towns lay in ruins, and no fewer than 2,000 Indians lay dead. Some 20 years later, an American agent found the Cherokee still traumatized. Elders had passed down tales of the horror, and the mere sight of an American was enough to terrify many children.

The bloody campaigns of 1776 all but knocked the Cherokees out of the war, and in May of 1777, Cherokee leaders sued for peace. But one breakaway faction of the tribe moved their towns west to Chickamauga Creek in northwestern Georgia where they remained fiercely defiant. Led by an indomitable young war leader named Dragging Canoe, these so-called Chickamauga Cherokees continued raiding the hated American settlers for an entire decade after the formal end of the war.

The Creek—alarmed by the Cherokee catastrophe—tried hard to maintain neutrality. But in the summer of 1780, Creek warriors were pressed into service in answer to British pleas for aid in storming Augusta in Georgia. They also fought alongside the British at Savannah in the winter of 1781-1782, when that city was under siege. The highly respected Creek war chief Emistesigo lost his life attempting to break through the American fortifications. Other southeastern tribes also fought on behalf of the British, but with lesser consequences. Shortly after Emistesigo's death, the British withdrew from the South and surrendered.

The southeastern Indians awaited the first actions of the victorious Americans with trepidation. The Treaty of Paris, which officially acknowledged colonial independence and ended the Revolution, placed most of the South in American hands. Florida was returned to the Spaniards. Not a single Indian tribe was mentioned in the peace treaty. In the decades to come, the native peoples of the Southeast would meet repeatedly with officials of the new nation, trying to find a way to live on the land together.

As its first diplomatic overture to the southern tribes, the fledgling United States government invited the leaders of the Choctaw, Chickasaw, and Cherokee peoples to a number of conferences at Hopewell, South Carolina, to outline future relations. The three nations signed treaties officially recognizing the U.S. victory over Britain and agreed to accept American protection. The Creek, however, who were invited to a separate meeting in Georgia, refused to sign.

The Creek desire to maintain independence was given force by the efforts of Andrew McGillivray. The son of a Scottish trader and a Creek woman who belonged to the prestigious Wind Clan, McGillivray had achieved the rank of beloved man, a Creek title traditionally reserved for elders of outstanding merit. Although McGillivray's clan lineage was important to his success, he was also well educated and possessed an excellent knowledge of white society, thanks to years of schooling in Charles Towne. When the war ended, many Creeks looked to him for leadership. McGillivray's greatest dream was to forge a unified nation. This, he felt, would provide the strength the Creek peoples needed to deal with the emerging American government. But such a notion ran completely counter to Indian custom. Although powerful leaders had arisen over the preceding 100 years, the Creek, like other tribes, still vested authority in their town headmen. While McGillivray labored to bring the towns together, rival headmen undercut his efforts.

Meanwhile, McGillivray worked to establish a partnership between the Creek Confederacy and the Spaniards. He believed that such an alliance would reinforce Creek independence, and as a result of his efforts, the Creek signed a treaty with the Spaniards in 1784. According to its terms, Spain recognized the Creek Confederacy and agreed to provide guns, ammunition, and other goods. For a time, McGillivray opposed any Indian alliance with the Americans. In 1786, when he learned that the Chickasaw, who had also made a pledge to Spain, were entertaining an American delegation, he sent warriors to intercede. But the Chickasaw struck an agreement with the Americans anyway, initiating bad blood with McGillivray and the Creek.

McGillivray was an astute observer of the political scene. He knew that the Creek could succeed only as long as their nemesis, the state of

Made of woodchuck hide with pieces of deer tail for ears, the Cherokee mask above represents the power of the wildcat. Masks such as these were worn during hunting rituals as well as by hunters stalking wild turkeys.

Georgia, remained isolated and weak. As he watched the United States move toward a constitutional system with greater centralization of power, he recognized potential danger for his people. If, for example, the entire United States were to align behind the claims of Georgia, Creek sovereignty would be in jeopardy. In 1790, one year after the ratification of the U.S. Constitution, McGillivray moved to preempt that possibility. He traveled to New York City, which by that time had replaced Philadelphia as the seat of government. There he managed to convince officials that the previous treaties signed between Georgia and compliant Creek headmen were fraudulent; he then succeeded in negotiating a new accord that recognized and guaranteed the borders of the Creek nation. For his part, McGillivray ceded three million acres of land. In a secret clause of the treaty, he became a brigadier general in the U.S. Army.

For the next few years, McGillivray continued his efforts to unite the Creek peoples. But his health, never strong, had been shattered by the strain of travel. The Creek leader died prematurely, in 1793, while still in his early thirties. McGillivray had never succeeded in attaining his goal—the creation of a unified Creek nation—and his death left the Creek without strong leadership. In the coming decades, the confederacy would be increasingly rent by internal dispute.

During this time, other tribes were also struggling to come to terms with changing politics, both at home and in their dealings with whites. The Chickasaw, for instance, divided their loyalties between the Spaniards and the Americans. One faction, which had formerly been friendly with the French, now turned to Spain for goods and protection. Leaders of the movement visited New Orleans, where they spoke with the Spanish governor. Meanwhile, however, another body of Chickasaws encouraged American traders to settle in among them.

For a while, the divided loyalty of the Chickasaw worked to the tribe's advantage. Just as the British and French had once wooed different headmen, Americans and Spaniards now vied for favors. Agents of both countries offered the Indians gifts of tobacco, blankets, rum, knives, hatchets,

WILES OF THE FISHERMAN

Artful hunters and experts at gathering plant foods, the people of the southern woodlands were also ingenious fishermen. The region abounded in rivers and coastal flats, and these waters teemed with a huge variety of fish—from bass, shad, sunfish, perch, and other relative small fry to sturgeon measuring eight feet long and catfish weighing 100 pounds and more. Here was a limitless supply of protein ready year-round to be caught and eaten.

Taking advantage of this bounty, the Indians of the Southeast, most notably the Creek, invented a wealth of sophisticated ways to snag their prey, employing traps and weirs, dams and nets, lines with hooks made of turkey bones, and spears with sharp points from the tails of horseshoe crabs. They even used a special poison that stunned the fish but did not harm their human consumers. A contest with a mammoth sturgeon required muscle power rather than ingenuity—a common way to catch these scaly giants was to lasso their tails and hang on to the rope.

Hip deep in an Oklahoma stream, three Creek fishermen dump a toxic powder into the water in one of a series of photographs taken in the 1920s. The photos show tribesmen using an ancient fishing method the Creek brought with them from their southeastern homeland to the Indian Territory.

Plunging into the stream, a dozen men and boys help spread the poison powder, made from the roots of an herb called devil's shoestrings—"Tephrosia virginiana." The herb paralyzed the fish, making them float to the surface where they could easily be caught.

Indians used this 15-foot-long log to distribute a fish poison called buckeye root. The depressions in the log were filled with the poison in the form of a paste; then the log was set afloat in a stream, where it gradually released the paralyzing toxin into the water as it moved with the current.

A Cherokee fish trap made of trimmed branches allowed the fish to swim through the opening but kept them from escaping. The Indians frequently placed traps such as these at the end of V-shaped dams that funneled fish into the openings.

Wading in the shallows, a Creek man grasps his catch in one hand while holding in the other a bow and arrows. Such weaponry was commonly used for fishing in clear, shallow waters where the prey could easily be seen.

and sometimes guns and powder. The Spanish presence gradually diminished, however. In 1795 Spain relinquished claim to a large parcel of land to the United States, and in 1800, they returned the territory of Louisiana to France. Although the Spaniards continued to hold Florida, they no longer wielded much authority there. Consequently, the Americans stepped up pressure on the Indians to cede their lands.

During the years since the Revolutionary War, the new nation had developed a coherent Indian policy. In essence, the goal was to acquire Indian land as quickly and cheaply as possible. This, it was determined, could best be done by encouraging the Native Americans to adopt a market economy and, in particular, commercial agriculture. Once Indian men learned to farm, raise livestock, and repair tools like the white men, the argument went, they would no longer need vast tracts of wilderness for hunting. It would then be easy to persuade them to sell surplus hunting grounds in order to earn money to invest in their farms or to buy more consumer goods.

The Indians were in no condition to resist. In 1801 the Chickasaw signed a treaty allowing the United States to create a road through their territory. Five years later, the tribe relinquished a major tract north of the Tennessee River. In exchange, they received $20,000, a considerable portion of which was held back to pay existing debts. The Choctaw accepted similar deals. At the turn of the 19th century, the tribe had endured a severe drought. Hungry and destitute, they too approved the wagon road. In their weakened state, the Choctaw also handed over two million acres for the paltry sum of $2,000. The following year they gave up a smaller parcel of land north of Mobile, opening the gates for a flood of American settlers. Encouraged, the U.S. government intensified pressure on the tribe, and in 1803 and 1805, the Choctaw signed away another five million acres.

The Cherokee seemed best able to adapt to the American policy. Perhaps because they had only recently been savaged in two devastating wars with the whites, the tribe accepted with less resistance American attempts to assimilate them. The U.S. government constructed a model farm on Cherokee land and taught the Indians how to use plows, spinning wheels, and looms. The farm included a blacksmith and a miller, so Cherokees were able to have their tools repaired and their wheat ground at home. Missionaries set to work trying to convert the Cherokees to Christianity, an enterprise that met with mixed success. The missionaries also

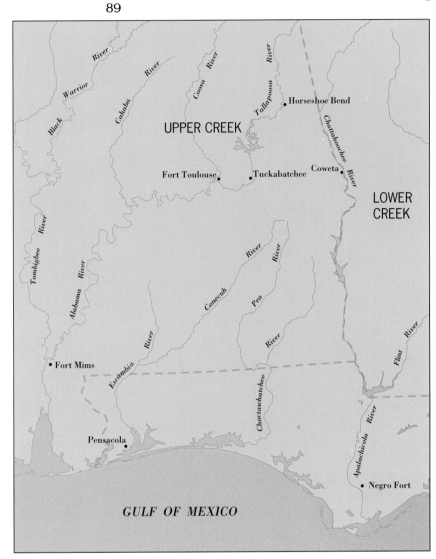

The Creek War broke out in 1813, when Upper Creek, or Red Stick, warriors staged the brutal massacre of settlers and their Indian allies at Fort Mims. Fighting soon raged across the Creek lands shown here until Andrew Jackson crushed the uprising at the Battle of Horseshoe Bend in March 1814. Many of the surviving Red Sticks fled south to Florida, where their presence precipitated an army attack on Negro Fort and a war with the Seminole.

established schools, where Cherokee children learned English, arithmetic, and geography. Although Cherokee parents often had qualms about losing their children to foreign ways, they seemed to understand that only by acquiring the tools of white civilization would the tribe be able to deal effectively with the United States in years to come.

As a consequence of their willingness to adapt, the Cherokee Nation experienced a return to prosperity. The tribe created a central government that had the power to overrule town councils. The tradition of blood revenge for crimes was abandoned and judicial power vested in the new government. Even laws of inheritance were changed. Traditionally, a Cherokee man willed his property to his sister and her children so that his wealth stayed within his clan. Under the new system, Cherokee law guaranteed that a wife would inherit her husband's wealth at his death, an innovation that did much to break up clan ties.

The Creek proved more stubborn when confronted with the prospect of change. After McGillivray's death, the United States sent an agent, Benjamin Hawkins, to live among the Creek and attempt to educate them in

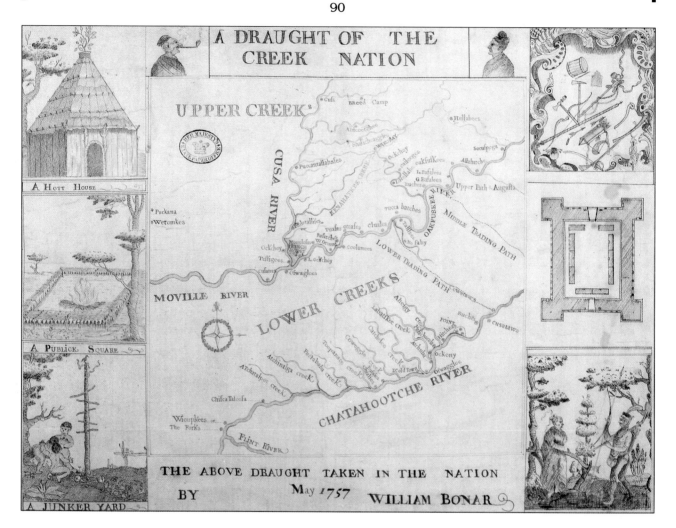

the ways of white people. Hawkins had some success in achieving McGillivray's dream of a unified Creek government. But when he suggested that Creek men take up farming—traditionally a female task—he met resistance. Even so, a number of towns, largely among the Lower Creeks in Georgia, complied. Most of the Upper Creeks bitterly resented Hawkins. In this corner of the Creek world, trouble was brewing.

In the fall of 1811, the Upper Creeks held their annual meeting in Tuckabatchee, on the lower Tallapoosa River. Among the 5,000 Creeks present, anger against the Americans was at a peak. Also in attendance was the great Shawnee war chief Tecumseh. He had come from his homeland above the Ohio River in the hope of enlisting the southeastern tribes in a great pan-Indian confederacy. The charismatic Shawnee gained a following among a group of young Creek medicine men. Called "prophets" by the whites, they claimed to possess a special understanding of the good and evil spirits occupying the traditional Creek three-tiered universe of earth, sky, and underworld, and they advocated a return to traditional ways. When Tecumseh departed for the north, some of these prophets accompanied him and spent the winter absorbing his doctrine. Returning home in the spring of 1812, they encountered a group of white settlers in west-

Commissioned by the British, this 1757 map of the Creek homeland shows the locations of the Upper and Lower Towns as well as their trade routes. Rare scenes depicting Creek life illustrate the borders of the map.

ern Tennessee and murdered them. These killings, and others in the Ohio country and within Creek lands, triggered a chain of events that led to war and, ultimately, devastation for the Creek. First, under orders from the federal government, Benjamin Hawkins demanded the arrest of the warriors responsible for the settlers' deaths. Creek leaders were permitted to send their own lawmen to bring in the culprits. But instead of taking the perpetrators into custody, the Creek officers summarily executed them. Militant factions in the tribe swore vengeance and set out to eliminate from the confederacy every last shred of white civilization.

In the summer of 1813, an observer noted that the "whole of the upper towns have taken up the war club." Since these war clubs were painted red, those who wielded them became known as the Red Sticks. The Red Stick crusade spread rapidly. By July the Red Sticks had slain nine Creeks who backed accommodation with the Americans, burned several villages, and destroyed livestock, fences, plows, and most everything nontraditional they came across, except for weapons. Most of the opposition to the

Creek Red Stick warriors, who advocated a return to Indian ways, are depicted slaughtering whites and Indians at Fort Mims on August 30, 1813. The massacre provoked the intervention of the United States, changing the Creek civil war into an all-out conflict between the Red Sticks and the Americans.

A NIGHT OF CHEROKEE RIBALDRY

One of the highlights of the winter ceremonial season for the Eastern Cherokees comes in the form of the boisterous and bawdy ritual known as the Booger Dance. The night air vibrates with anticipation as guests come together at the home of a sponsor to perform the sacred and social dances that are associated with the season. Suddenly a gang of four or more rowdies, all of them sporting masks with exaggerated human features, barges into the house. Coughing and growling, and pretending to speak in foreign tongues, these so-called boogers begin chasing the women and pantomiming lewd behavior—to the vast amusement of the assembled audience.

When their identity is questioned by the host, the boogers—many of whom boast obscene names—reply that they hail from "far away" or "across the waters." They then demand women and a fight, but agree to settle for a dance. Af-

ter more buffoonery, the boogers are joined by female partners, who serenely ignore the maskers' sexually suggestive movements. The boogers then disappear into the night, and the traditional dance cycle resumes.

This ribald ritual has been interpreted by some Indians as symbolizing the intrusion into the Cherokee world of crude, uninvited outsiders. Indeed, many of the masks—several of which are featured on the following pages—are caricatures of Europeans and other non-Cherokees. The act of parodying them perhaps serves to somehow diminish their threat to the community.

Shuffling counterclockwise around an upright length of timber, masked booger dancers perform their burlesque in a painting by Cherokee artist Murv Jacob.

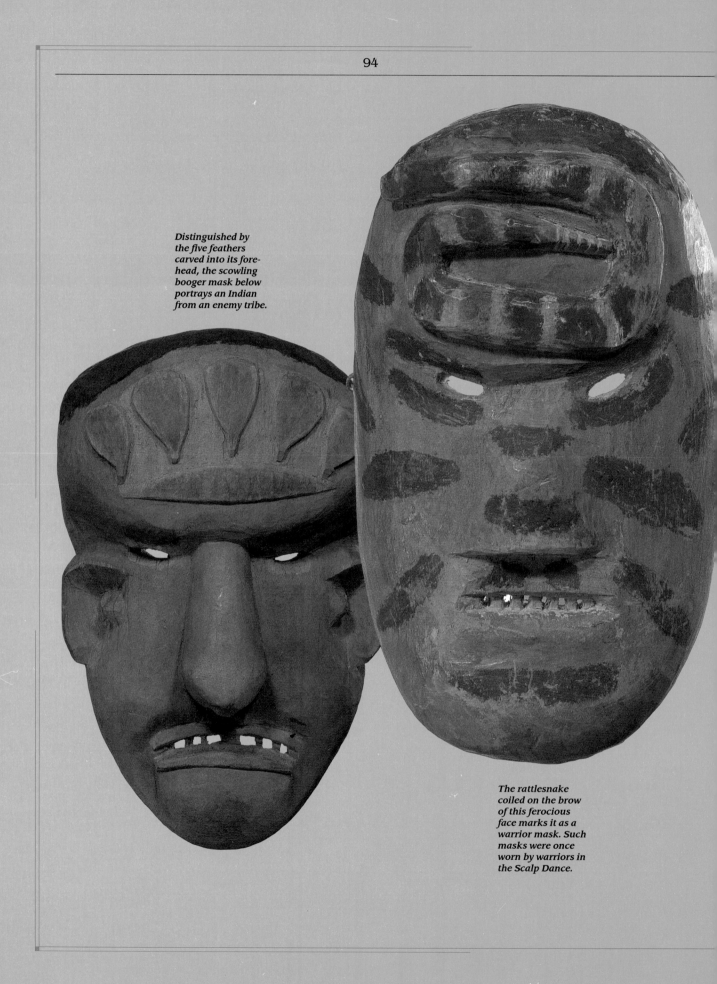

Distinguished by the five feathers carved into its forehead, the scowling booger mask below portrays an Indian from an enemy tribe.

The rattlesnake coiled on the brow of this ferocious face marks it as a warrior mask. Such masks were once worn by warriors in the Scalp Dance.

With its bushy eye-
brows and shock of
fair hair—actually
glued-on fur—the
mask shown below
mimics the pale vis-
age of a white man.

Topped by a fur hat
with earflaps, this
mustached mask
represents another
white man, possibly
a French trader.

Symbolic of a "mean creature"—as well as a diseased white man—this booger mask was fashioned from a wasp nest. The eyeholes were carved, while the nest's natural exit serves as the mouth.

With its fur-rimmed phallic nose constructed from a gourd neck, this mask typifies the bawdy spirit of the booger ritual.

Opossum fur decorates this charcoal-colored mask, a representation of a black man. The comblike teeth carved into the image reinforce its menacing mien.

Red Sticks came from the Lower Creek towns. It was led by William McIntosh of Coweta. Like Andrew McGillivray, McIntosh was born into the Wind Clan. He had embraced white ways to the fullest and lived the life of a wealthy southern planter and slave owner. McIntosh would join forces with an Indian named Big Warrior, leader of the Creeks from Tuckabatchee, the only upper town to oppose the Red Sticks.

Fueled by loss of land, economic disruption, resentment of the civilization program, but above all by traditional Creek religious values, the rebellion escalated swiftly. The Creek Confederacy became ever more deeply divided. At one point, a group of headmen opposed to the uprising took refuge with Big Warrior in Tuckabatchee. When the Red Sticks laid siege to the town, the headmen sent word to Benjamin Hawkins, who arranged for a party of Lower Creek warriors to rescue them. In the meantime, a band of Red Sticks traveled to Pensacola, where they purchased gunpowder from the Spaniards. On their way home, they were attacked by a combined force of whites and Creeks. Some Red Sticks died in the skirmish, and the Red Sticks once more vowed to retaliate in kind. They chose

A Cherokee woman grinds corn with a long wooden pestle, while another holds a child near their log cabin in North Carolina about 1890. From the mid-1700s, many southeastern Indians began building homes similar to those of the white settlers.

as their target Fort Mims, a well-protected plantation in southern Alabama, where the warriors who had attacked them had taken refuge, along with a number of their supporters and families. The Red Stick force, led by Red Eagle, also known as William Weatherford, totaled about 750 warriors. When the smoke cleared, some 250 men, women, and children inside the fort had been slaughtered.

The Fort Mims massacre was precisely the incentive the Americans needed to launch an all-out campaign against the Indians. Between the late summer of 1813 and the spring of 1814, troops from Tennessee, Georgia, and Mississippi swept through the Creek nation in a fury. At the head of the largest force—which included a band of Creeks under McIntosh and Big Warrior as well as some 600 Cherokees—was General Andrew Jackson of Tennessee. Twice Jackson led his forces into the heart of Creek territory, and twice his advance was checked, first by problems with his troops, next by fierce Creek resistance. Then, in March of 1814, Jackson encountered the Creeks at a neck of land on the Tallapoosa River known as Horseshoe Bend. Some 1,000 Red Sticks had barricaded themselves behind strong breastworks. But Jackson's force was well armed and perhaps two or three times greater in number. While his Indian allies swam the river to threaten the Red Sticks from the rear, Jackson launched a frontal assault. The fighting lasted all day. When it ended, approximately 800 Red Sticks lay dead. Many of Jackson's men stripped the skin from the bodies as gruesome souvenirs of the battle. Weatherford, who had miraculously escaped capture a few months earlier by jumping his horse off a bluff into a river, was not among the dead. He had been off inspecting other fortifications on the day of the attack.

The war shattered the Creek nation and claimed 3,000 lives—approximately 15 percent of the total population. Jackson's campaign had swept most of Upper Creek country clean and driven as many as 2,500 Creeks into Florida where they sought refuge among the Seminole. Jackson continued his advance down the Tallapoosa River and built Fort Jackson on the ruins of the old French redoubt, Fort Toulouse. In August of 1814, the Creek leaders assembled there to have a treaty dictated to them. They were shocked by its terms, spelled out by Jackson himself. The Creek Confederacy would be forced to give away a huge tract of land—more than 23 million acres, representing roughly half of their domain. In an ironic note, it was the progovernment William McIntosh and his lieutenants who had to do the signing—most of the Red Stick leaders were either dead or in Florida, waiting for the next round of fighting. ◆

THE TRAIL WHERE WE CRIED

In bedraggled processions stretching to the horizon, the Indians struggled westward, leaving their homeland behind them. Unlike the white settlers who had journeyed in the same direction, eagerly seeking gold or a bright new beginning, the Native Americans had no choice—theirs was a forced migration into uncertain exile in the vastness beyond the Mississippi River.

As a result of the Indian Removal Act of 1830, each of the five major southeastern tribes faced emigration. The policy, endorsed by President Andrew Jackson as a means of making room for white settlement, engendered bogus treaties that compelled the Indians to swap their ancestral lands for a place in the Indian Territory—present-day Oklahoma. Removal cost the Indians not only their roots but also thousands of lives sacrificed to disease, hardship, and rebellion.

None suffered greater losses than the Cherokee. Regarded by whites as the most advanced of the so-called Five Civilized Tribes, the Cherokee had emulated the white man's form of government and education in the hope that whites would leave them alone. But in 1838, nearly 17,000 Cherokees were rounded up and held in stockades. Then, in 17 separate groups, they were launched on the 1,000-mile journey westward. The images on these pages, together with the remembrances of participants and others, evoke an ordeal so sorrowful that the Cherokee called it The Trail Where We Cried.

The map pinpoints landmarks in the Cherokee migration from Georgia and nearby states to what is now Oklahoma. Although some traveled by riverboat, most trekked overland via Tennessee, Kentucky, Illinois, Missouri, and Arkansas.

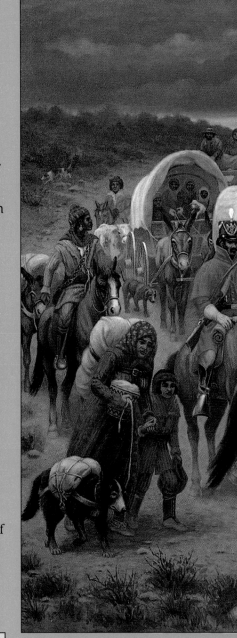

In the painting above, dispirited Cherokees move westward under armed escort by the tribe's own warriors and federal soldiers.

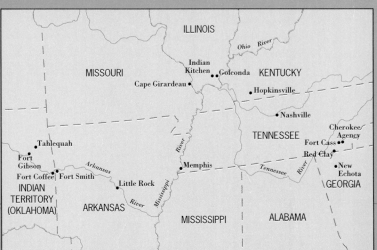

ILLINOIS

Ohio River

MISSOURI

Indian Kitchen • • Golconda   KENTUCKY

Cape Girardeau •

• Hopkinsville

• Nashville

TENNESSEE

Cherokee Agency

Fort Cass • •

Red Clay •

• Tahlequah

Arkansas River

• Memphis

Tennessee River

• New Echota

Fort Gibson •

Fort Coffee • Fort Smith •

Little Rock •

INDIAN TERRITORY (OKLAHOMA)

ARKANSAS

Mississippi River

GEORGIA

MISSISSIPPI

ALABAMA

An iron cooking pot like this one was supposed to be issued to each family, along with a blanket for every individual. But amid the chaos of what the Cherokee called the "drive away," many had to do without.

LEAVING IT ALL BEHIND

"The most brutal order in American warfare"—as one soldier who was there described it—began with mass arrests. "When the soldiers came to my house, my father wanted to fight," recalled Rebecca Neugin, "but my mother told him that the soldiers would kill him if he did, and we surrendered without a fight. She brought what bedding and few cooking utensils she could carry and had to leave behind all of our other household possessions." Everyone was detained in camps where many Indians died from disease during the months before departure. A missionary who witnessed one group head west wrote, "It is mournful to see how reluctantly these people go away; even the stoutest hearts melt into tears when they turn their faces toward the setting sun."

With its shutters and mullioned windows, the tribal Supreme Court Building at the former Cherokee capital of New Echota, Georgia, shows white influence on architecture as well as political institutions. The Cherokee moved their capital to Red Clay, Tennessee, in 1832 after Georgia outlawed most gatherings.

A panoramic view near Boone, North Carolina, typifies the Blue Ridge region, which extends into northern Georgia and eastern Tennessee and constituted the ancestral Cherokee heartland before removal.

As depicted at right, the U.S. Army conducted a roundup of Cherokees during the spring of 1838. "Women were dragged from their homes," wrote Private John Burnett. "Children were often separated from their parents and driven into the stockades, with the sky for a blanket and the earth for a pillow."

OVERLAND IN DESPAIR

The first leg of the overland route lay through Tennessee, home of the former president and one-time friend of the Cherokee, Andrew Jackson, whose Indian Removal Act was responsible for their plight. Farther along, in Kentucky, an aged Cherokee who had once served in battle under Jackson recognized a white comrade from the days they had spent suppressing Indian rebellions. "I then thought Jackson my best friend," the Cherokee told him. "But ah! Jackson does not serve me right. Your country does me no justice now!"

The anguish of the Cherokees was palpable, recorded a traveler from Maine who came upon a group in Kentucky: "The Indians as a whole carry on their countenances everything but the appearance of happiness. Some carry a downcast, dejected look bordering upon the appearance of despair; others a wild frantic appearance as if about to burst the chains of nature and pounce like a tiger upon their enemies."

The painting below reflects the misery that soon engulfed the emigrants. "Many of the aged were suffering extremely from fatigue," wrote a white man who was traveling in Kentucky. "Several were quite ill, and an aged man was in the last struggles of death."

CHOHAWK 1957

The trail in Kentucky trod by Cherokees still bisects this forest near Hopkinsville. Rebecca Neugin noted they "got so tired of eating salt pork that my father would walk through the woods as we traveled, hunting for turkeys and deer to feed us."

Mantle Rock (top left), a 40-foot sandstone arch in Kentucky, shielded Cherokees as they trekked westward.

Across the Ohio River in Illinois (left), another ancient campsite, Indian Kitchen, afforded shelter and water from Lusk Creek.

Burdened by the sick and their own fatigue, early-rising emigrants follow the sun's morning path in this painting by Cherokee artist Robert Annesley.

A RELENTLESS PACE OF MARCH

Every morning the march went on regardless of weather or infirmity. The pace was so relentless that women who were ready to give birth had to be left by the wayside. A story told to Margaret Brazel by her grandmother related: "They were left alone, out in the woods, to give birth, and they were expected to catch the group after the birth. No one was allowed to stay with them or go back to look for them." Some of the women never returned—victims, it was believed, of wild animals. Many babies also failed to survive. On December 14, 1838, Daniel Buttrick, a white missionary with the Cherokees, wrote: "Last night a child about 14 months old died. This is the 15th death since we crossed the Tennessee River."

An occasional act of kindness temporarily eased the heartbreak of exodus. When a group of Cherokees showed up at the door of Mrs. Jasper Buel of Golconda, Illinois, she shared with them the pumpkin she was cooking.

STALLED BY THE ELEMENTS

At the Mississippi River, some Cherokee groups found great chunks of ice clogging the ferry crossings and had to camp in bitter cold until the passage was clear. Survivors later recounted the "miseries of that halt beside the frozen river, with hundreds of sick and dying penned up in wagons stretched upon the ground, with only a blanket overhead to keep out the January blast."

During a month-long delay on the Illinois bank of the Mississippi River, Jesse Bushyhead, a Cherokee Baptist minister, lost a daughter to illness. But after crossing, his wife gave birth to another, who was appropriately named Eliza Missouri. At Little Prairie, Missouri, Evan Jones, a white missionary, felt disheartened by weather and distance. The cold was so intense, his group sent ahead a "company every morning, to make fires along the road, at short intervals" to warm the way. "We have now been on our road 75 days and have traveled 529 miles. We are still nearly 300 miles short of our destination."

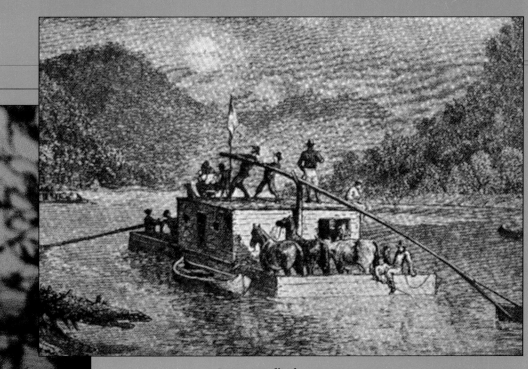

The photograph at left shows the part of the Mississippi River where some emigrants had to wait for weeks until ice cleared and allowed passage from Illinois to Cape Girardeau, Missouri.

Groups traveling by water plied the Tennessee, Ohio, Mississippi, and Arkansas Rivers in dangerously crowded steamboats or in small, flat-bottomed craft like the one shown above.

In the painting below by Cherokee artist Murv Jacob, emigrants pause to pay respects to a fallen comrade. Some Cherokee Christians carried Bible verses printed in their own phonetic alphabet.

The Arkansas River—shown here near Fort Smith on the western border of Arkansas—was the gateway to the Indian Territory for Cherokees who were arriving by boat.

NEW HOME ON THE PRAIRIE

The last major group of emigrant detachments emerged onto the tall-grass prairie of the Indian Territory in March 1839. Of the approximately 17,000 Cherokees arrested for removal, perhaps one-fourth—about 4,000—had not survived. Among the dead was the wife of John Ross, principal chief of the Cherokee Nation.

Resilient in tragedy, Ross went on to help rebuild his people's shattered culture and foster peace with their neighbors. But Ross's resentment burns through a complaint of continued mistreatment addressed to Congress in 1840: "When our eastern country was lately taken from us without the consent of the majority, and the great mass of our people captured, they said that it was hard, but they were the weaker, and would not resist. They were doubted, but not a hand was raised and now, those who have survived are in the West. We have done our part. We have given up all. What has been done by the United States. Nothing."

A far cry from the mountains and woodlands they had left behind, the prairie of the Indian Territory became the new home of most of the exiled Cherokees.

Indians from more than a dozen tribes gathered at the enormous council convened by the Cherokee in June 1843—four years after removal—to promote friendship in the region. Some 10,000 delegates attended the gathering in the new Cherokee capital of Tahlequah.

3

NATIONS ON THE MOVE

A young Seminole (left) sits for his portrait wearing the garb of a western cowboy. The last of the principal southeastern tribes to complete relocation west of the Mississippi River, the Seminole did not begin to adopt white styles of dress until the mid-1850s.

On February 12, 1825, near Jackson, Georgia, an influential Creek of mixed ancestry named William McIntosh met with federal commissioners at a tavern he owned called the Indian Springs Hotel and signed what amounted to his own death warrant. The document was a treaty requiring the Creek peoples to cede all of their territory in Georgia and most of their land in Alabama. In exchange, the Creek would receive $400,000—scarcely five cents per acre—along with expenses for their removal to the unknown country west of Arkansas that would become identified as the Indian Territory. The commissioners who negotiated this fateful deal with McIntosh and his followers were acting in defiance of President James Monroe, who had flatly rejected the notion that one small faction of Creeks could fairly represent the entire tribe. McIntosh, for his part, was on even shakier ground than the commissioners in accepting their terms. Seven years earlier, the Creek National Council—an assembly of leaders to which McIntosh belonged—had decreed that anyone selling Creek land without the council's approval would be subject to execution. A Creek chief named Opothle Yoholo, who was present during the negotiations but refused to sign the treaty, forcefully reminded McIntosh of the consequences. "My friend, you are about to sell our country," he declared. "I now warn you of your danger!"

McIntosh would soon be called to account, for shortly after President Monroe left office in March, the U.S. Senate would ratify the spurious Treaty of Indian Springs. In risking death at the hands of outraged Creeks, McIntosh was motivated by profit and a longstanding desire to accommodate the whites. Half of the $400,000 payment would go to him and a few hundred of his associates; in addition, he would be paid the inflated sum of $25,000 for his tavern and two nearby tracts of land.

McIntosh closely identified with white authorities. Born in 1775 to a Creek woman and a British officer serving as an agent to the Indians, he had learned to speak and write English as a child and later modeled himself after the ambitious white planters who were transforming the South. In addition to his tavern, which was purchased with the help of former Georgia governor David Mitchell, he acquired two plantations, worked by scores of slaves. By 1825 he had three wives—one Creek, one Cherokee, and one of mixed heritage.

McIntosh owed his privileged position partly to the military alliances he had forged with whites during the Indian conflicts that convulsed the region during the early 1800s. When Upper Creeks—the Red Sticks—rose up in 1813, McIntosh was among the Lower Creeks who resisted them and aided General Andrew Jackson in his successful campaign to crush the uprising. The grateful Jackson called McIntosh the "bravest man I know" and appointed him brigadier general. After the end of the Creek War, McIntosh remained a trusted aide of Jackson's as the future president embarked on an offensive against the Seminole, who were harboring escaped slaves and fugitive Red Sticks in the woods and glades of northern Florida. McIntosh joined in the offensive in the hope that he and his followers would garner booty and root out the 1,000 or so Red Sticks who had fled to Florida with their families.

In July 1816, Jackson lit the fuse for this Seminole War by ordering an attack on a fort located on the Apalachicola River in the Florida panhandle, 15 miles upriver from the Gulf of Mexico. Established by the British when they went to war with the United States in 1812 and evacuated in 1815 with the end of the war, the bastion had been left to a small number of Seminoles and fugitive Creeks and some 300 blacks, whose presence led whites near the Florida border to label the stronghold the Negro Fort. General Jackson and American traders considered the fort a menace to shipping, and slaveholders upriver claimed the blacks as their property and demanded their return.

Infringing on Spanish territory, Jackson sent a flotilla of four boats up the Apalachicola from the Gulf while a ground force of army regulars and Indian allies—including 150 Lower Creeks led by McIntosh—descended on the fort from Georgia. Soon after the attack began, a hot shot from one of the gunboats struck the bastion's main powder magazine and blew the fort apart. In an instant, recollected one witness, scores of lifeless bodies "were stretched upon the plain, buried in sand and rubbish, or suspended from the tops of the surrounding pines." McIntosh's warriors overran the smoldering ruin and quickly subdued the survivors. Captive slaves were trussed up and marched off to toil on plantations in Alabama and Georgia.

The angry Seminoles and Creeks and their black allies bided their time. Then, in November 1817, they took revenge by ambushing a boat headed up the Apalachicola with federal troops and members of their families, killing some 40 soldiers and a number of their kin. In response,

Creek headman William McIntosh earned the enmity of his people by negotiating in 1825 the Treaty of Indian Springs, which allowed the United States to gain possession of most of what remained of Creek land in Georgia and Alabama.

Andrew Jackson marched into Florida to war on the Seminoles and their black comrades in arms. During the spring of 1818, McIntosh and a force of nearly 2,000 Creek warriors provided a mighty assist to Jackson's force as they assailed the Seminoles, putting their villages to the torch, executing some of their leaders, and enslaving captives, black and Indian alike. Jackson, intent on securing Florida for the United States, did not relent until he had captured the Spanish capital of Pensacola in May. Spain agreed in 1819 to cede Florida to the United States for $5 million. The Seminole, who had no say in the transaction, were soon pressured into surrendering 28 million acres of relatively fertile ground in northern Florida. In return they received less than one penny an acre and a small reservation in central Florida, consisting of four million acres of swamplands and sandy pine barrens later described by the Seminole agent William DuVal as "by far the poorest and most miserable region I ever beheld."

After this Seminole War, McIntosh profited from victory by shipping home cattle and slaves from Florida to be placed on the auction block in Georgia. He even tried unsuccessfully to persuade the federal government to treat the Seminoles as Creeks so that he and the Creek National Council could benefit from any compensation the Seminoles received for their lands. Later, as a paid employee of two white Georgians serving as U.S. treaty commissioners, he sought to bribe Cherokees into selling their land in the northern part of Georgia. The Cherokee Council expelled him and warned the Creek in writing to keep a close watch over McIntosh, or "he will ruin your Nation."

When details of the Treaty of Indian Springs became known in 1825, many Creeks concluded that McIntosh had indeed brought them to ruin. The Creek National Council publicly ousted him from their ranks, then met in secret session and sentenced McIntosh and several of his associates to death. On April 29, a band of some 200 "lawmenders"—as the Creeks who enforced tribal edicts were known—set out for the Georgia plantation where McIntosh was staying with others who had been condemned. Leading the avenging lawmenders was a battle-scarred old Red Stick named Menawa, who had suffered much for opposing the victorious Americans during the Creek War and had never forgiven McIntosh for aiding them. Late the following night, he and his followers surrounded McIntosh's house. After allowing relatives and guests of the treaty makers to depart unharmed, they set the building afire and waited for the offenders to emerge. McIntosh fled from the flames and stumbled into a lethal hail of gunfire. Long after he died, the lawmenders continued to pour bullets into him, as if intent on destroying all that he represented.

The slaying of McIntosh dramatized the dissension that racked the southern tribes as they came under mounting pressure from white Americans to surrender their homelands. In contrast with the obliging white traders of earlier times, the planters and homesteaders who spread out across the Southeast in the early 1800s had little use for the Indians. So strong was the tide of settlement that it overwhelmed even the numerous Creeks. Between 1810 and 1820, the non-Indian population of Alabama alone increased more than twelvefold to 128,000, compared with a total Creek population in that state and neighboring Georgia of perhaps 20,000.

In the face of this onslaught, some Indian leaders concluded that there was nothing to be gained by opposing removal and came to terms with authorities. But others clung to their territory and defied the treaty makers. Factional strife intensified, threatening the solidarity of proud native peoples who aspired to nationhood.

In the case of the Creek, their forceful repudiation of McIntosh and the document he signed won them a fleeting concession from Washington. For the first time, the federal government revoked a treaty it had imposed on Indians and offered them a better deal. In 1826 the Creek peoples won the right to retain their territory in Alabama in return for agreeing to sell their land in Georgia. Many Creeks later moved from Georgia to Alabama, while some chose to emigrate west of the Mississippi—chief among them followers of Roley McIntosh, William's half brother. All the while, however, support was growing in the nation's capital for a policy that would end such piecemeal measures and sweep all Indians from the Southeast.

The acknowledged champion of Indian removal was Andrew Jackson. Long before he became president in 1829, Jackson advocated the voluntary relocation of eastern tribes to lands west of the Mississippi River to make way for white settlement. President Thomas Jefferson had laid the groundwork for that policy in 1803, when he engineered the Louisiana Purchase and doubled the territory of the United States, providing ample room for the resettlement of eastern Indians. It remained for Jackson, however, to make Indian removal a reality. Far from being an Indian hater, he had adopted a young Creek boy whose parents were killed by his soldiers and raised him as a son at the Hermitage, his plantation outside Nashville. Yet expelling Indians from the Southeast benefited Jackson and his backers both financially and politically. Before invading Florida, for example, he advised friends and relatives that land values there would soon go up, and some of them profited as a result. Jackson's aggressive efforts to open up Indian lands for settlement won him a devoted following among white southerners who were hungry for holdings.

In order to satisfy that demand, Jackson had personally negotiated several treaties with the southern tribes—first with the Creek after he put down the Red Stick uprising in 1814, and later with the Cherokee, Choctaw, and Chickasaw. Both the Cherokee and Choctaw treaties provided for an exchange of eastern tracts for land west of the Mississippi. Altogether, the cessions negotiated by Jackson accounted for about half the

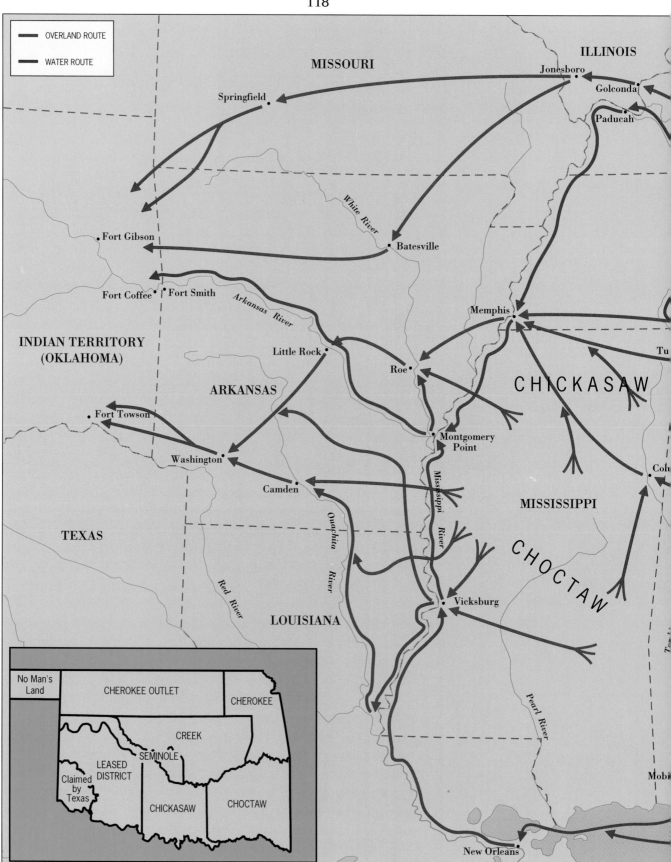

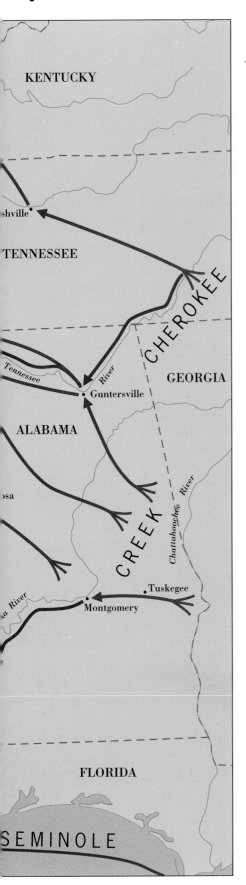

The map at left traces the main removal routes, collectively known as the Trail of Tears, of the so-called Five Civilized Tribes from their ancestral lands in the Southeast to their new homes in the Indian Territory (present-day Oklahoma). During the principal removal period in the 1830s, some 60,000 Native Americans took part in the trek westward. The inset shows the boundaries of the five nations as they existed from 1855 until the end of the Civil War.

territory held by those four groups before the Creek War. Like other negotiators, Jackson combined threats with incentives to bring chiefs around. As he put it later, agents seeking concessions from Indians must appeal "to their fears and indulge their avarice."

During the 1820s, however, resistance to removal increased among the southern tribes. The opposition came not only from traditionalists, who spurned the intruders' customs and felt a sacred bond to the land of their ancestors, but also from Indians who were adopting white ways and believed that they were entitled to the houses they built and the fields they cultivated. Increasingly, Indian men were giving up hunting and becoming farmers, while their wives confined themselves largely to domestic chores. Throughout the region, villagers invited missionaries to establish schools to teach agriculture and other vocations. By 1825 the Choctaw alone had 13 schools of their own, and a few graduates even went on to college in the North. Most Indians in the area adopted some form of Christianity, without necessarily forsaking their tribal rituals. In many places, community leaders discouraged acts of blood revenge and organized roving mounted patrols that served as police.

As Indians assimilated elements of white culture, they were better prepared to challenge the claims outsiders made on their lands. The Cherokee, for example, succeeded in spelling out their rights—thanks to a phonetic alphabet, or syllabary, introduced in 1821 by a crippled craftsman named Sequoya. By devising a symbol for each of the 85 syllables in the spoken language, Sequoya made it possible for thousands of Cherokees to become literate with a few days of study. An influential tribal newspaper, the *Cherokee Phoenix,* began weekly publication in 1828, printing in alternating columns of Cherokee and English such vital information as the laws of their nation. Those laws had been codified in 1827 during a constitutional convention at the newly established Cherokee capital of New Echota in the contested area of northern Georgia. The resulting document, modeled closely on the U.S. Constitution, provided for executive, legislative, and judicial branches. It also defined the boundaries of Cherokee territory within the states of Georgia, Alabama, Tennessee, and North Carolina—and declared the Cherokee Nation "sovereign and independent."

To white Georgians, in particular, the new Cherokee constitution posed a serious threat. Resentment had long festered there because the federal government had yet to fulfill an agreement it made in 1802 to buy up all Indian territory within the state's projected boundaries if Georgia in turn would relinquish claims to its western territory (the future states of

Alabama and Mississippi). Now the Cherokee were asserting their sovereign right to retain their land. The Georgia legislature reacted late in 1829 by extending the state's jurisdiction over all Cherokees and others, such as missionaries, who were living there. Subsequent legislation abolished Cherokee government, prohibited Cherokees from testifying against whites in court, and denied the Indians the freedom of speaking out against removal.

Other southern states enacted repressive laws during this period. Tennessee passed anti-Cherokee measures, Mississippi cracked down on the Choctaw and Chickasaw, and Alabama victimized the Creek. Although legislators invoked states' rights to justify these laws, their true purpose was to make the lives of Indians so miserable that they would gladly emigrate. Yet by 1830, despite pressures that had been building for more than a decade, only a fraction of the native population in the Southeast had voluntarily moved west—perhaps 2,500 Creeks and roughly twice as many Cherokees and Choctaws.

The blow that ultimately dislodged the vast majority of Indians in the region came not from the states but from federal legislation advanced by Andrew Jackson in 1829—the year that "the Devil became President," as one Choctaw put it. That December, President Jackson repudiated the Cherokee claim of sovereignty and urged Congress to approve his landmark Indian Removal Act.

Aimed principally at the southern tribes, that bill empowered the president to renegotiate earlier treaties, such as the one guaranteeing the Creek their land in Alabama, and to impose new deals that would remove tribes beyond the Mississippi. The ensuing debate, one of the bitterest in American history, raged for weeks in Congress and was echoed in the nation's press and town meetings. Jackson and others promoted removal as a humanitarian act to "preserve this much injured race," as he put it. Only through resettlement far from the corrupting influence of whites, they claimed, could the Indians improve their lot—an argument that ignored the considerable strides groups such as the Cherokee had made in their eastern homelands. Opponents of the legislation protested that it was reprehensible to overturn earlier treaties and launch a fresh round of manip-

The federal government attempted to protect the tribes residing in the Indian Territory from unscrupulous traders by forcing white merchants to procure a permit, like the one above, from the Office of Indian Affairs. Despite the law, unlicensed peddlers continued to plague the Indians, selling illegal whiskey and worthless nostrums.

Tribal boundaries within the Indian Territory were distinguished by obelisk markers, like the one at right. The markers stood about six feet tall and also served as No Trespassing signs in an attempt to keep out unauthorized whites.

ulative deal making. In May 1830, Congress narrowly approved the act; in the House of Representatives, the margin was only five votes.

On the face of it, the Indian Removal Act did not compel Indians to cede their homelands. It authorized the president to set aside tracts west of the Mississippi for reception of such tribes "as may choose to exchange the lands where they now reside, and remove there." The tracts were in the region designated as the Indian Territory, whose boundaries roughly coincided with those of present-day Oklahoma. Tribes emigrating there would receive moving costs, compensation for improvements they had made on their old lands, and a year's subsistence in the West. Theoretically, tribes had the option of rejecting any treaty. But the act offered them no protection from repressive state laws. Furthermore, President Jackson felt free to ignore opponents of removal and negotiate with tribal leaders who appeared receptive to a deal, using funds appropriated by Congress to reward those who cooperated. In truth, the act exposed Indians to official coercion on an unprecedented scale.

Jackson pushed forward almost immediately, determined to bring about removal by fair means or foul. In September treaty commissioners met near Dancing Rabbit Creek in eastern Mississippi with a large number of Choctaws led by Greenwood LeFlore. Like William McIntosh, the 30-year-old LeFlore was a prosperous planter, the son of a French-Canadian trader and a Choctaw woman. But unlike McIntosh, he could make some claim to speak for his people as a whole: He had recently maneuvered to get himself elected as their principal chief, the first Choctaw ever to be so designated. Although he himself planned to retain his Mississippi plantation with the blessing of white authorities, he advocated a sweeping treaty of removal for the Choctaws.

Federal officials stage-managed the treaty council in an effort to distract the Indians from the business at hand. They admitted to the council grounds all manner of white gamblers, saloon keepers, and prostitutes for the entertainment of the expected 6,000 Choctaws, but banned the missionaries who might protest the revelry or the government-imposed settlement. Some Choctaw leaders at first balked at the treaty but came around after being tempted with offers of cash and threatened with military intervention. The council finally agreed to exchange the remaining Choctaw territory in Mississippi, some 10 million acres, for 15 million acres in the southern half of the Indian Territory.

The Choctaw thus became the first to embark upon what came to be

THE GIFT OF WRITTEN LANGUAGE

A hero to his people, the Cherokee farmer and craftsman named Sequoya single-handedly devised the first system for writing an Indian language. Born about 1770 in a village in present-day Tennessee, Sequoya had no formal schooling and knew no English. But he realized that English-speaking people with the black marks they made on paper had a huge advantage, being able to both preserve ideas and transmit them to one another in writing. Vowing to give the Cherokee the same benefit, he labored for a dozen years beginning in 1809 to perfect a system of 85 symbols that expressed all the spoken syllables of his tribe's complex tongue. Miraculously, his syllabary proved so easy to learn that within a few years, thousands of Cherokees could read. And first one newspaper and then another used Sequoya's symbols to help unite the embattled tribe, despite white persecution and expulsion from their homelands.

A copy of his syllabary hanging on the wall behind him, Sequoya sits for a portrait wearing a large silver medal awarded by the federal government. He received many honors, one of which was having the stately redwood trees of California named for him.

Sequoya lived in the tiny cabin at left after moving west to the Indian Territory in 1818. When he was working on his syllabary, some of his fellow Cherokees, misunderstanding his solitary endeavors, mocked him for neglecting his farm and accused him of practicing witchcraft.

An edition of the Cherokee Phoenix from July 1828 prints news in English in the two left columns, and in Sequoya's syllabary on the right of the page.

A Portion of the Cherokee Phoenix, July 9, 1828

Printers set type for the Cherokee Advocate, successor newspaper to the Phoenix that was published in the Indian Territory after the Cherokees were forced westward in the 1830s. Like the Phoenix, the Advocate appeared in both English and Sequoya's Cherokee.

Seated outside his cabin, Sequoya tests his newly made syllabary by teaching it to his young daughter. The scholar died in 1843, at about the age of 73, while on a long, exhausting trip to Mexico to locate a band of Cherokees that had fled there from white persecution.

called the Trail of Tears. The term embraced not only the heartbreak and humiliation of being uprooted from ancestral lands but also the misery many had to endure on the way westward. Most of the Choctaws left in three yearly migrations beginning in October 1831, making the long journey from Mississippi through Arkansas and on to the Indian Territory by steamboat and by wagon in some cases, but mostly on foot. The treks were poorly planned by the federal government. Severe early-winter weather subjected the first group to exposure; an epidemic of cholera decimated the second migration. Of the nearly 15,000 Choctaws who emigrated during this period, as many as 2,500 died during the journey or soon thereafter. The tribe paid heavily in other ways as well. Sale of the lands ceded in Mississippi brought the federal government $8 million, more than enough to cover all the costs associated with the removal.

Some Choctaws were so embittered by the loss of their land and the dismal prospect of the journey west that they were tempted to fight removal. But tribal leaders drew on their authority and on lessons learned from Christian missionaries to discourage violence. A Choctaw named James Culberson recalled the words of his grandfather, Kanchi, who in 1834 urged members of his band to set aside their anger and make a new start in the Indian Territory.

"My own kin and blood brothers, I know how you feel about what has happened to you," he declared. "I too have felt the same and looked about for comfort from this wretchedness.

"Some time back," Kanchi went on to say to his fellow tribesmen, "I heard a man preach from a book that he called a Bible [Holisso Holitopa], and although that book was read by a white man, I believe there is something better in it than the way the white man acts. We are in much trouble now, but don't want to kill or destroy, so give us hearts that we hear about in this book and let us be good, and if we live to see this new country to which we travel, help some of us to do good to those we meet. Perhaps we will not bring shame upon the land."

Sadly, more than a few of those listening would not live to see that new country. Kanchi himself died in the act of rescuing some Choctaws whose raft capsized while they were crossing the Mississippi.

As many as 6,000 Choctaws declined to embark on that perilous journey and remained in Mississippi under state authority. By Article 14 of the Treaty of Dancing Rabbit Creek, they were to receive grants of 640 acres or more upon registration with the Indian agent. But the agent, William Ward, was corrupt and incompetent. Thanks to him, few Choctaws succeeded in registering for grants. The vast majority who stayed behind were left landless and endured living conditions worse than those of most black slaves. In time, many of them made their way westward to join the Choctaws in the Indian Territory.

In the meantime, Greenwood LeFlore, who had orchestrated the treaty, prospered on a Mississippi delta plantation that eventually grew to 15,000 acres and was worked by 400 slaves. Although he was deposed as chief by his own people, LeFlore went on to represent his county in the state legislature, where he sometimes offered colleagues glimpses of his Indian heritage. He once grew so exasperated at a pompous legislator who insisted on making his entire speech in Latin that he took to the floor and spoke for an hour in Choctaw.

The Choctaw's northern neighbors, the Chickasaw, did not begin the process of removal until 1837, although they were the first to sign such a treaty, in August of 1830, with President Jackson himself looking on. The delay in enactment was the result of a clause in the treaty that left it to the Chickasaw to find land in the Indian Territory that they deemed suitable for their new home. After a long search, the Chickasaw paid the Choctaw $530,000 for occupancy rights to the western two-thirds of the Choctaw holdings in the Indian Territory. That deal was financed through the sale of Chickasaw land, much of which was auctioned off publicly to benefit the people as a whole. The proceeds also went to equip the more than 4,000 Chickasaws who finally moved west in 1837. Wagons were piled high with furniture, farm tools, and other useful equipment that eased the burdens of relocation. Accompanying the Chickasaws were more than 1,000 black slaves, who moved west with their masters. Colorful processions of emigrants—the Chickasaw men in turbans and sashes and the women with elaborate curls stacked high—wound their way toward the Indian Territory by wagon and by riverboat.

In Alabama, meanwhile, many Creeks were so intent on avoiding removal that their leaders agreed to an unusual treaty. Although the agreement ceded more than half the tribe's 5.2 million acres in exchange for land in the Indian Territory, it reserved 320 acres in Alabama for each Creek family, which could then decide whether to sell the plot and move at government expense or remain on it subject to state laws. To maintain this foothold in their homeland, the Creek were required to sacrifice their age-old custom of communal ownership of property. But leaders hoped that most families would adhere to their allotments and work with their Creek neighbors in order to preserve native villages.

As it turned out, the Creek came under relentless pressure to surrender their allotments. Federal officials failed in their treaty promise to keep intruders away from lots reserved for Creeks; some 10,000 whites moved in during the next two years and proceeded to wrest land from the Indians by force or deprive them of their holdings by fraud. In one notorious scheme, a land speculator would hire an Indian for a pittance to pose as the owner of a particular allotment and swear before a government agent that he had sold it to the speculator. The speculator then sold the property to a white settler, who would drive the rightful Creek owner off the land. Because Alabama law banned Indian testimony in court, Creek victims of such fraud had no legal recourse. "I have never seen corruption carried on to such proportions in all of my life before," remarked one observer. "A number of the land purchasers think it rather an honor than a dishonor to defraud the Indian out of his land."

Even Indian outrage was manipulated to benefit the intruders. Deprived of their land, some Creeks were reduced to begging door to door or eating bark from trees, and little was required to incite them to violence. In May 1836, hundreds of Creeks went on a rampage, burning houses, setting fire to a toll bridge across the Chattahoochee River, and ambushing a stagecoach and killing the passengers. This fitful uprising was supported by a defiant 84-year-old chief named Eneah Emathla, and it took on the inflated name of the Second Creek War. In fact, some of the incidents were provoked by whites anxious to divert an ongoing federal investigation of the land frauds. One white man was later sentenced to hang for inciting the attack on the stagecoach. An editorial in the *Montgomery Advertiser* went so far as to claim that the so-called war was "all a humbug, a base and diabolical scheme, devised by interested men, to keep an ignorant race of people from maintaining their just right, and to deprive them of the small remaining pittance placed under their control."

Yet the violence was enough to provide the Jackson administration with a pretext for ending the investigation of the land frauds and ordering the prompt removal not only of those involved in the uprising but of all the Creeks remaining in Alabama. Eneah Emathla's followers were ferreted out by an army of 11,000 men, including regular troops, vigilantes, and some 1,800 Creeks, whose leaders bore a grudge against the old chief and hoped to placate white authorities. By July Emathla and 800 of his men had been rounded up and were being herded toward the river port of Montgomery in manacles and chains, with their wives and children trailing behind. "Old Eneah Emathla marched all the way, handcuffed and

The inherent dignity, character, and courage of the southeastern Indians shine through in these portraits by George Catlin, shown at right and on the following pages. Catlin made the paintings at Fort Gibson, the U.S. Army military center for the Indian Territory, in the mid-1830s when the subjects of his art were enduring a wretched existence in their unfamiliar prairie home.

THE BLACK COAT, CHEROKEE MAN

TCHOW-EE-PUT-O-KAW, CREEK WOMAN

SNAPPING TURTLE, ALSO KNOWN AS PETER PITCHLYNN, CHOCTAW MAN

SAM PERRYMAN, CREEK LEADER

chained like the others," wrote one witness. "He never uttered a complaint." As the procession approached Montgomery, one Indian cut his own throat. Another clubbed a guard to death and was shot down on the spot. Then the warriors and their kin—some 2,500 people in all—were loaded aboard steamboats for a grueling journey that took them westward along the Gulf Coast and upriver to the Indian Territory. Scores died along the way of dysentery and other ills.

The remaining Creeks fared no better. During the following months, army troops rounded up all but a small number of fugitives and prodded them westward. Some journeyed by boat, while others trudged overland through Tennessee and Arkansas, a trek that required up to three months. Many set out in the fall and ended up walking shoeless and nearly naked in the December cold. "In this destitute condition, they are wading in cold mud, or are hurried on over the frozen ground," reported one journalist. Many died of sickness or exposure, he added, and were left by the road, "covered only with brush." In addition, hundreds of Creeks who traveled by boat perished through the neglect of a private company contracted to provide transport. The contractor chartered old paddleboats and crammed them with Indians. In October 1837, one such boat, manned by a drunken crew, steamed up the wrong side of the Mississippi, collided with another vessel, and sank, killing 311 Indians. In all, the emigration and its bitter aftermath may have cost the lives of 3,500 Creeks. "Our road has been a long one," lamented one Creek chief after the trek, "and on it we have laid the bones of our men, women, and children."

Removal was perhaps an even greater tragedy for the Cherokee, for in addition to great loss of life, they suffered a severe blow to their national pride and unity. Of all the native peoples who resided in the region, they had progressed the most toward organizing themselves in ways that whites advocated. As John Ridge, a prominent Cherokee orator, declared to a northern audience: "You asked us to throw off the hunter and warrior state: We did so. You asked us to form a republican government: We did so—adopting your own as a model. You asked us to cultivate the earth, and learn the mechanic arts: We did so. You asked us to learn to read: We did so. You asked us to cast away our idols, and worship your God: We did so."

Crucial to Cherokee hopes of avoiding removal was their claim of sovereignty—their right to defy restrictions placed on them by states and deal with the federal government from a position of strength. To establish their sovereignty, the Cherokee went all the way to the Supreme Court. In 1832, in the case of *Worcester* v. *Georgia,* they challenged a law requiring all whites living in Cherokee territory to swear an oath of allegiance to the state. For defying that statute, one Samuel Worcester and a fellow missionary to the Cherokees had been arrested by the Georgia Guard and imprisoned. The Supreme Court under Chief Justice John Marshall ruled in favor of the Cherokee, repudiating Georgia's authority over their territory. Cherokees celebrated in the belief that they were at last free from state coercion. But neither Georgia—which refused for many months to release the two missionaries—nor the federal government would honor this ruling. "John Marshall has made his decision," President Jackson was quoted as saying, "let him enforce it now if he can."

Disillusioned, a minority of Cherokees concluded that they would be better off in the Indian Territory. They soon found a leader in the person of Major Ridge, father of orator John Ridge. As former speaker of the Cherokee Council, Major Ridge retained considerable influence with John Ross, the principal Cherokee chief since 1828. Although Ross was only one-eighth Cherokee and Ridge was nearly full blooded, the two men had much in common. Both had fought for Andrew Jackson against the Red Sticks during the Creek War, in which Ridge earned the rank that he retained as part of his name. Both were prosperous plantation owners who lived in elegant mansions in northern Georgia only a mile or so apart, where each operated a ferry and maintained dozens of black slaves. And both were staunch opponents of removal—until Ridge broke with Ross and challenged his right to represent the Cherokee peoples in their dealings with the federal government.

Ridge's change of heart came at a critical moment. Despite the Supreme Court ruling, the state of Georgia went ahead with a plan to distribute Cherokee land within its borders to white settlers in a mammoth lottery. In 1832 hundreds of winners in the lottery attempted to occupy the tracts they had bought, often with violent results. Earlier that same year in Washington, President Jackson had met with Major Ridge's son and told him to go home and advise his people "that their only hope of relief was in abandoning their country and removing to the West." Jackson's appeal helped sway Major Ridge, who converted to the cause of removal along with his nephew, Elias Boudinot, founding editor of the *Cherokee Phoenix.*

The Cherokee split into two factions: Ridge's pro-removal Treaty Party and Ross's much larger National Party. Although both factions sincerely

This political cartoon shows President Andrew Jackson as the Great Father, toying with a contingent of tiny southeastern Indian wards. Jackson's advocacy of the Indian Removal Act of 1830 sparked bitter opposition among many northern liberals, and Congress passed the legislation by only a narrow margin.

believed that their respective positions would benefit the people, the chasm that developed between them quickly widened. Ross implied that his opponents were traitors and forced Boudinot to resign his position as editor of the *Cherokee Phoenix* by banning all pro-removal writings. Threats surfaced against the lives of leaders on both sides, and several assassinations were reported. Georgia officials promoted further disunity by exempting both Boudinot and the Ridges from any eviction measures that might be brought on by the lottery. Ross, on the other hand, came home from Washington one day in 1835 to find his plantation in the hands of the lottery winner who claimed his holdings. He moved his family across the border into a log cabin in Tennessee. The following year, Georgia militiamen crossed the state line, arrested Ross at bayonet point, and held him for nine days until his rival, John Ridge, helped win his release.

Despite this magnanimous gesture, the conflict soon passed beyond hope of reconciliation. In December 1835, a U.S. treaty commissioner summoned the entire Cherokee Nation to New Echota, warning that all who failed to attend would be regarded as approving the actions taken there. Of a population of more than 18,000, only a few hundred Cherokees, led by Major Ridge, showed up. They approved a treaty that had already been rejected in its essentials twice that year by the Cherokee. It called for their removal from lands east of the Mississippi within two years in exchange for $5 million and seven million acres in the Indian Territory. Among the signers was John Ross's own brother, Andrew. Major Ridge was mindful of the tribal law that made unauthorized disposal of land a capital crime, an edict similar to the one that had led to the execution of William McIntosh. As he made his mark on the treaty—he had never learned to write in English—Ridge said, "I have signed my death warrant."

The Treaty of New Echota gave Andrew Jackson, now serving his second term as president, an excuse to press ahead with the removal process. Despite petitions of protest containing the signatures of some 15,000 Cherokees—and objections from a tribal delegation that the treaty was "false upon its face, and against the known wishes of the Nation"—the U.S. Senate ratified the pact in May of 1836, by a margin of just one vote. Jackson dispatched federal troops under General John Ellis Wool to keep order among the Cherokee and prepare them for removal. Wool wrote that he found the duty heartrending, especially the sight of whites eyeing the Cherokees like vultures, "ready to pounce upon their prey and strip them of everything they have."

Through it all, John Ross remained resolute. He made repeated trips to Washington to lobby against removal, gathered more petitions of protest, and even toyed with the idea of a Cherokee migration to Mexico or to

British-held Oregon. Even though he was only partly Cherokee, spoke the native language haltingly, and never learned Sequoya's syllabary for writing it, Ross identified wholeheartedly with his people. Followers called him Tsan Usdi, or Little John, because he was just five feet six inches tall. Yet he loomed large in the eyes of most Cherokees, who trusted in him to protect their interests.

Ross's influence kept to a minimum the number of Cherokees who decided to emigrate voluntarily—although Major Ridge and some 500 of his followers left in March 1837, followed by several other small groups totaling no more than 1,500. As the removal deadline approached in May of 1838, nearly 17,000 people clung to their homelands. Determined to oust them, Jackson's successor, President Martin Van Buren, dispatched Major General Winfield Scott with 7,000 troops and the authority to call up state militiamen. Scott's grim task was to round up the Cherokees and impound them in 23 log stockades built for the occasion. When all had been detained, they would be marched to river landings in Tennessee and Alabama for deportation westward.

The roundup began on May 26 and lasted 25 days. With rifle and bayonet, squads of soldiers scoured the fields and hills. Cherokee men were seized from behind the plow, women dragged from their homes, and entire families plucked from the dinner table and sometimes separated. Troops were under orders from General Scott to act with civility, but there were inevitable instances of brutality. Private John G. Burnett, who had grown up near the Cherokees in Tennessee and took part in the roundup, recalled that in one home where a child had just died, the family was whisked away before the body could be interred, "leaving the child in the cabin. I don't know who buried the body."

Typically, the Cherokees who were hurried off to the stockades had time to take only the clothing on their backs. Their houses, furnishings, and livestock fell prey to whites who followed the roundup squads. Those

Swiss artist Karl Bodmer captured the tragic plight of displaced Choctaws during his travels to the lower Mississippi River region in 1833. His watercolor sketches of a refugee camp (left), an Indian named Billie (above, left), and a forlorn family (above) support his description of the Choctaws as "living in a sadly inactive condition."

Although only one-eighth Indian by ancestry, John Ross became the leading advocate of Cherokee independence. As leader of the majority National Party that opposed removal, Ross served as principal chief from 1828 until his death in 1866 at the age of 75.

scavengers looted homes and rifled graves, stripping the corpses of silver pendants and valuables. Some of them carried out their depredations before the Cherokees had even been driven out of sight. In the stockades, disease spread rapidly, killing hundreds of people. A Georgia volunteer who later served as a colonel in the Confederate army said many years afterward, "I fought through the Civil War and have seen men shot to pieces and slaughtered by thousands, but the Cherokee removal was the cruelest work I ever knew."

After a few thousand Cherokees had been shipped off, federal authorities agreed to a proposal from John Ross and the Cherokee Council that they supervise their own migration at a cost to the government of just $66 per person. Ross organized the remaining Cherokees and black slaves into contingents of 1,000 people or so. Each contingent would have a complement of white physicians and Cherokee police to maintain order and would be equipped with horse-drawn wagons to carry provisions and the infirm. About 1,400 Cherokees would remain behind, either because they were exempt from removal under previous local agreements or because they had eluded the roundup; most of the fugitives retreated to the mountains of western North Carolina.

Although the Cherokee gained some control over the removal process, they could not postpone it. They had little choice but to set out in October on a trek that would require at least three months. Once again, thousands of ill-equipped Indian exiles would be subjected to winter weather. Contingents of Cherokees departed for the Indian Territory a few days apart, following routes through Tennessee, southern Illinois, Missouri, and Arkansas. "It was like the march of any army," observed one witness, "regiment after regiment, the wagons in the center, the officers along the line, and the horsemen on the flanks and at the rear." The marchers were not seasoned soldiers, however, but civilians of all ages vulnerable to disease and exposure.

A Cherokee man later spoke for many of the exiles in his broken English and enduring anguish. "Long time we travel on way to new land," he recalled. "People feel bad when they leave Old Nation. Womens cry and make sad wails. Children cry and many men cry, and all look sad like when friends die, but they say nothing and just put heads down and keep on go towards West." Along the trail, this Cherokee buried his father, mother, and five brothers and sisters: "One each day and all are gone." Years later, he could still hear in his mind the moaning from the wagons that carried the frail, the sick, and the dying.

As November gave way to December, conditions worsened. Heavy rains mired the exiles in ankle-deep mud, ice blocked them from crossing rivers for days on end, and diseases took an increasing toll. "I have known as many as 22 of them to die in one night of pneumonia due to ill treatment, cold, and exposure," noted John Burnett. Among the 4,000 Cherokees who per-

Major Ridge (opposite page, right), a leader of the small, pro-removal Cherokee faction known as the Treaty Party, believed that the only hope for tribal survival lay in accepting the U.S. government edict to move west. In 1839, four years after Ridge signed the Treaty of New Echota that exchanged Cherokee land for a tract in the Indian Territory, anti-removal nationalists assassinated him, along with his son John (left) and his nephew Elias Boudinot (far left), the first editor of the Cherokee Phoenix.

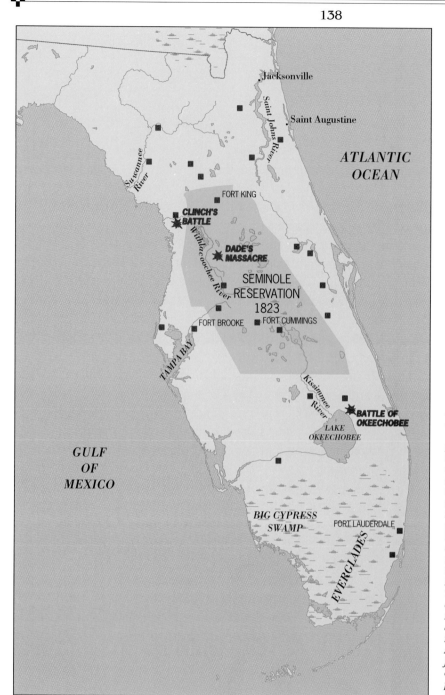

For seven years, between 1835 and 1842, the Florida peninsula was the site of bloody guerrilla warfare, as the defiant Seminole thwarted every attempt by the U.S. military to expel them. The fighting began when the government brought in troops to remove the Seminole to the Indian Territory. The Seminole, however, proved to be masters of ambush and mobility, and in the end, the Americans were forced to rely largely on attrition and political subterfuge to subdue them.

ished during the removal process was John Ross's wife, Quatie. After giving up "her only blanket for the protection of a sick child," Burnett reported, "she rode thinly clad through a blinding sleet and snowstorm, developed pneumonia, and died in the still hours of a bleak winter night."

The leading Cherokee contingent did not arrive in the Indian Territory until January 4, 1839. The last group limped in on March 24. Removal had cost the Cherokee much more than anticipated. For years afterward, John Ross tried to persuade the government to make up the overrun of $37 per person, which amounted to well over $500,000 for the entire nation.

A more pressing account was settled promptly without his knowledge. Soon after reaching the Indian Territory, some of Ross's followers met on their own and invoked the law against unauthorized land sales violated by Major Ridge and his kin. On June 22, 1839, the enforcers ambushed Ridge, his son John, and his nephew Boudinot at separate locations and put them to death for betraying the nation.

Even the passionate opposition to removal evidenced by the Cherokee paled beside that of the Seminole, who continued to harbor Red Sticks and fugitive blacks after their war with Andrew Jackson's forces came to an end. For all their diversity, these peoples shared bitter memories of that conflict and dreaded being uprooted again. Rather than submit, they banded together to launch one of the most remarkable wars of resistance in American history. In that struggle, a force of no more than 1,500 warriors would bog down overwhelming numbers of state and federal troops in the swamps and sweltering heat of the Everglades for nearly seven years.

Here as elsewhere, the trouble began with spurious removal treaties. In 1832 and 1833, a group of chiefs from the reservation in central Florida signed a pair of documents that required the Seminole to cede their Florida lands for two cents an acre and move to the Indian Territory within three years. Bribes and coercion figured in the negotiations, and many Seminoles denounced the treaties.

The rising anti-removal fervor coalesced around a young warrior called Osceola, a name derived from the Muskogee *asi-yahola,* meaning "black drink singer." Born in Alabama about 1804, he was the son of a Creek woman who married an English trader named William Powell—who may have been Osceola's natural father or his stepfather. After the end of the Creek War, Osceola and his mother made their way to Florida in the company of a group of militant Red Sticks. He became a familiar figure around Fort King, site of the Indian agency that oversaw the Seminole reservation. Elegant in his dress and renowned both for his physical grace and for his passionate rhetoric, Osceola was an inspirational figure for a displaced people who cared less for a leader's hereditary credentials than for his commanding presence.

Whites too recognized Osceola's potential. The U.S. agent to the Seminole, Wiley Thompson, deliberately cultivated his friendship, even presenting him with a custom-made rifle. But Osceola's ardent opposition to removal angered Thompson, and in the spring of 1835, the agent jailed

Osceola was a prisoner at Fort Moultrie not far from Charleston, South Carolina, and was suffering from a high fever and severe sore throat when George Catlin painted this portrait of him. The great Seminole war leader died on January 30, 1838, the day after Catlin left the fort.

him for six days for his outspokenness. "The agent has had his day," Osceola reportedly vowed as he was led away, "I will have mine."

With the removal deadline set for January 8, 1836, troops began mobilizing at Fort Brooke at the head of Tampa Bay, and Osceola urged Seminole warriors to take up arms. In late November of 1835, he and a dozen followers shot to death a Seminole chief who had signed the removal treaties. A month later, on December 28, Osceola and his men ambushed agent Thompson and an army officer outside Fort King. At least one of the balls that riddled Thompson was fired from the rifle he had given Osceola. Taking his victim's scalp as a trophy, Osceola then rode south with his band to rendezvous with a much larger Seminole war party that had just surprised and annihilated two companies of soldiers under Major Francis Dade who were bound for Fort King to aid in the forced removal. Of the 108 troops who had come under attack, only three had survived, and two of them later died of their wounds.

Osceola took charge of the exultant Seminoles, gathered up some more fighting men, and soon proved himself as a war leader in a pitched battle with troops led by General Duncan Clinch, whose aim was to sub-

This colorful calico shirt is purported to have been worn by Osceola on the day of his death. He was about 34 years of age at the time.

due the defiant Indians by attacking their villages on the south bank of the Withlacoochee River. Crossing the river on December 31, General Clinch blundered into a trap laid by Osceola, who wore an army officer's coat and joined in the fighting himself, suffering a slight arm wound. His determined followers killed four soldiers and wounded 59, and deflected Clinch from his planned assault.

Osceola emerged from this battle as the Seminole's principal war chief as well as their leading spokesman. A few weeks later, he wrote a defiant letter to General Clinch with the help of Abraham, a black leader who served also as interpreter and scribe. Seminole resistance, he vowed, might last five years, or "until the last drop of the Seminole's blood has moistened the dust of his hunting ground."

This Second Seminole War presented a novel challenge for the U.S. Army—guerrilla warfare. Although that term was of recent vintage, having been coined to describe Spanish partisans whose hit-and-run attacks helped drive Napoleon's occupying troops from Spain in 1814, such tactics were nothing new for the Indians of Florida. For countless generations, native war parties had been stealing up on their enemies and inflicting

swift punishment before melting away into the swamps. Such bewildering raids by warriors armed with bows and lances had set back several early Spanish expeditions to the area, and American forces were destined to suffer many similar reversals at the hands of Osceola's men. The federal troops seldom saw the Seminoles until they attacked, their bodies painted red and black, letting loose unearthly war cries that began like growls and ended with shrill yelps.

To the advantage of surprise, Osceola added that of mobility. His warriors—and the family members who often traveled with them—could decamp at a moment's notice. Their most substantial form of shelter was the simple open-sided chickee, but on the move, they might just sling hammocks. Such was the discipline of the kinspeople who accompanied the warriors that there were even reports of mothers smothering their babies to silence crying that might give away their whereabouts.

Thousands of white soldiers—regulars and volunteers from neighboring states—were dispatched to Florida to campaign against the Seminole warriors, and they loathed every moment of it. They marched in foul-smelling water up to their armpits, stumbled over hidden cypress stumps, and slogged through saw grass sharp enough to slash through their boots. By night, they heard wolves howl and panthers scream and, by day, feared alligators and rattlesnakes almost as much as the Indians who might be lurking in the next stand of pine trees. Yet their deadliest enemies were

Impenetrable swamps such as this section of the Everglades served as sanctuaries for Seminoles resisting U.S. Army efforts to drive them out of their Florida homeland. The region's abundant supply of game, fish, and wild plants kept the Indians from starvation.

Two Seminole men in a canoe made from a hollowed-out log prepare to pole down one of the Everglades' countless waterways. Their ancestors used the same type of craft to elude federal troops.

dysentery, malaria, yellow fever, and other diseases, which killed more soldiers than Seminole bullets. As one rueful volunteer put it, "I have offered to do duty in Hades."

Their commanders came confident of quick victory. Major General Winfield Scott, one of the first, typified the dozen or so generals to face the Seminole. He arrived in February 1836 with a military band, three wagonloads of furniture, and dreams of subduing the enemy with a textbook campaign—one that called for three columns totaling 4,650 men to converge on Osceola's forces along the Withlacoochee. Instead, army supply wagons bogged down in the mud, and entire units became lost in the maze of swamp and forest. Weeks of campaigning claimed no more than 60 Indians. Not even the presence of 75 friendly Seminoles serving as guides saved Scott from embarrassment. By the end of the year, the army had abandoned most of its posts in the Florida interior.

In 1837, however, irregular tactics utilized by a new commander, Brigadier General Thomas Jesup, began to yield results. Jesup, better known as a quartermaster than a combat leader, understood that hunger could be a devastating weapon and set out to deprive the enemy of subsistence. He dispatched units to scour the countryside and drive Seminoles from their permanent villages or temporary camps. Then the troops burned the dwellings, killed or seized livestock, and destroyed crops and stores of the starchy coontie root from which the Seminoles made bread.

The Indians grew so hungry that women in a detention camp were seen picking up, kernel by kernel, the corn dropped by army horses.

Jesup also undercut a key source of the Seminole's strength—their black allies. Early in the war, these fugitives from plantations in Georgia and Alabama fought with special fervor alongside the Indians to avoid being captured and sent back to toil for white owners. But Jesup appealed to them by making it known that he would ship any blacks who surrendered westward to the Indian Territory. Several hundred accepted this inducement, and by the spring of 1838, blacks no longer played a significant role in the Seminole rebellion.

At the same time, Jesup used treachery against the Seminole, defending his tactics on the grounds that his opponents had no scruples when it came to warfare. He invited Seminoles to peace parleys under a white flag of truce, whereupon he seized them for shipment to the Indian Territory. Such duplicity brought Jesup his biggest catch of all in October of 1837, when Osceola sought a meeting to negotiate the release of King Philip, a leading Seminole chief who had been captured the previous month. Jesup dispatched Brigadier General Joseph Hernández and 250 horsemen to Osceola's encampment near Saint Augustine. While Hernández and Osceola talked under a white flag, army troopers surrounded the camp and seized the chief and 70 of his warriors without firing a shot. Osceola was put in chains at Saint Augustine. Afterward, he and several members of his family were taken north to Fort Moultrie at Charleston, South Carolina. A stream of white visitors came to visit the renowned prisoner—among them artist George Catlin, who painted two portraits of Osceola and talked with him at length.

Osceola soon fell gravely ill with quinsy, a severe throat infection. He refused the remedies of the presiding army physician, Dr. Frederick Weedon, and turned to a medicine man. On January 30, no longer able to speak, he signaled to his two wives to bring him his battle dress. He put on his deerskin leggings, calico shirt, war belt, bullet pouch, powder horn, and turban with three ostrich feathers. Then, as was Seminole custom before entering battle, he applied vermilion war paint to one side of his face and neck. Thus girded, he shook hands with the army officers and Seminole chiefs who had been summoned. "He made a signal for them to lower him down upon his bed, which was done," wrote Dr. Weedon. "He then slowly drew from his war belt his scalping knife, which he firmly grasped in his right hand, laying it across the other on his breast, and in a moment smiled away his last breath without a struggle or groan."

Osceola was buried with full military honors the following day—but not before Dr. Weedon had taken it upon himself to sever the dead man's head. The physician, who had conscientiously watched over Osceola during the period of his imprisonment, never explained his action, but it may have been an effort to preserve something of the famous man as a scientific curio. The public's fascination with Osceola only increased after his death. The war had grown more and more unpopular in the northern United States, and the departed Seminole warrior emerged as a symbol of freedom and defiance. In time, more than 20 towns and counties across the nation would bear his name.

In the swamps of Florida, meanwhile, the surviving Seminole warriors resisted more fiercely than ever. Even before Osceola's death, they had demonstrated their resolve in the largest battle of the war. On Christmas Day, 1837, with their war leader in prison, some 400 Seminoles faced a force more than twice as large, commanded by a future U.S. president, Colonel Zachary Taylor. Carefully deployed behind a morass of saw grass near Lake Okeechobee, the Indians put their scouts in trees to direct the fire while marksmen below notched the trunks to steady their aim. For nearly three hours, they held off wave after wave of soldiers who tried to advance through water and mud three feet deep. Taylor's futile assault cost him 26 dead and 112 wounded, while the Seminoles escaped with relatively few casualties.

This fresh setback for the army crushed any hope that the war would soon be over. In May of 1838, a weary Jesup transferred command to Zachary Taylor, now a general, who proposed an elaborate pacification scheme that would divide Seminole country into 20-mile squares and build a small fort in each. That plan proved overly ambitious, and Taylor eventually moved on to other challenges, leaving later commanders to try other approaches. One general dressed and painted his men like Indians to surprise some Seminoles. The governor of Florida even imported 33 bloodhounds used for tracking down runaway slaves in Cuba and set them on the Indians. Purchased for more than $5,000, the bloodhounds succeeded in sniffing out a grand total of two Seminoles.

In the end, hunger and fatigue sapped the strength of the Seminole warriors and their leaders. In March of 1841, the leader of one of the larger remaining bands, Coacoochee, made contact with officers at Fort Cummings in central Florida and vowed to surrender with his followers within a few months. When he later hesitated, a young lieutenant named William Tecumseh Sherman went after the chief and brought him in, shackled

hand and foot. "I feel the irons in my heart," Coacoochee said. Given a choice between death by hanging and a reward of $8,000 if he cooperated, he agreed to send messengers into the swamps to bring his people in. When October came, Coacoochee and 210 followers boarded steamboats for the long journey to the Indian Territory. Other bands soon trickled in, and the war sputtered to an end. In the final analysis, removing some 4,000 Seminoles from Florida had cost more than $30 million and claimed the lives of 1,500 white Americans and at least 1,000 Indians. Rather than expend any more lives to pry fugitives out of the Everglades, the army allowed several hundred Seminoles to remain there.

Among the last groups to surrender for emigration in 1842 were the 40 members of Chief Pascofa's band—Creeks who had taken refuge among the Seminoles six years earlier when troops forced their people from Alabama. As their boat steamed down the Ochlockonee River toward the Gulf and passed the market town of Port Leon, where whites lined the banks watching, Pascofa's followers, huddled in army blankets, received permission to utter one last ceremonial war cry. Afterward, the army colonel escorting them reported, a "revulsion of feeling seemed to

Choctaw riders called light horsemen maintained law and order in the new Choctaw territory. The light horsemen rode a circuit through the land, dispensing justice, the responsibility of the tribe's clans in pre-removal times.

Two Choctaw light horsemen (below) patrol a Choctaw town. The lawmen had the authority to serve as both sheriffs and judges. Perpetrators of minor crimes, like the man shown tied to the tree at right, were whipped. A serious offense, such as murder, was punishable by death.

overcome them." They fell silent, pondering what they had lost and what awaited them in the mysterious West.

The ordeal of removal forced nearly 60,000 members of the five major southern tribes to cope with the challenges of a strange new world. Arriving at their allotted territories, they faced unfamiliar terrain and the threat of raids from the Osage, Kiowa, Comanche, and other Plains Indians who felt no more kindly disposed to the displaced tribes than they did to white intruders. In the beginning, most of the emigrants crowded together in camps, where disease and hunger took a continuing toll. Over time, however, bands of Indians headed out to establish homesteads and villages, settling along rivers where they could raise corn and other crops and try to re-create the conditions that they had left behind.

Internal strife hindered attempts at a new start. Among the Creek, the followers of Roley McIntosh were already well established in the Indian Territory and did not welcome the other members of that nation who began arriving in 1836 under duress. Among the Cherokee, followers of the late Major Ridge rallied around his cousin, Stand Watie—who himself had barely escaped execution for signing the removal treaty—and clashed with the largest faction led by John Ross as well as a third faction called

the Old Settlers, who had made their way west two decades earlier. Fighting continued intermittently until 1846, when the three groups reached an accord by which Ross continued as principal chief of the Cherokee.

Despite such tensions, the new emigrants made remarkable progress over the years. They organized patrols to keep intruders from settling on their territory, although white traders and emigrants passed through unhindered. They set up businesses and expanded their ranches and farms; some Indians established plantations of more than 1,000 acres, worked by the black slaves who had accompanied them westward. The Choctaw used profits from their farms and stores to help finance the migration of more than 5,200 kinsmen who had remained behind in Mississippi. The Cherokee, after settling their differences in 1846, again took the lead in education with the help of missionaries. Outstripping their white neighbors in Arkansas, Missouri, and Kansas, they established a system of 126 public schools. It was during this period of renewal that the occupants of the Indian Territory came to be known as the Five Civilized Tribes.

Just as the bitter memories of removal were receding, the tribes became enmeshed in a new struggle—the Civil War. The outbreak of that conflict in 1861 reopened old wounds between rival parties in the Indian Territory and led to strife as deadly as that which afflicted whites in border states like Missouri. Early on, factions within all five tribes sought to ally themselves with the Confederates for a variety of reasons—including the natural inclinations of wealthy Indian slaveholders and the proximity of Confederate Texas and Arkansas, to which the five tribes had close ties. Other Indians stoutly resisted an alliance with the Confederacy, however. Some did so because they scorned slavery and the native slaveholders or because they remembered the bad treatment accorded them by leaders of

As the Indians became increasingly assimilated, their government buildings came to be indistinguishable from white equivalents. Shown here in late-19th-century photographs are the Chickasaw capital located at Tishomingo (left), the Creek capital at Okmulgee (center), and the Cherokee capital at Tahlequah (right).

the southern states. Others opposed any entanglement that would expose tribes to retribution by one side or the other.

In the spring and summer of 1861, a Confederate deputy named Albert Pike negotiated separate treaties with prominent members of the five tribes. As with the earlier removal treaties, these commitments were fiercely denounced by other tribal leaders, particularly among the Cherokee and the Creek. Leading the Creek opposition was the elderly Opothle Yoholo, who in 1825 had warned William McIntosh against dealing away Creek land. Although he himself owned many slaves, Opothle Yoholo advocated neutrality, and his plantation became a rallying ground for several thousand like-minded Creeks, as well as hundreds of slaves who fled from their Indian owners. Fearing attack, Opothle Yoholo decided to seek refuge in federal-held Kansas. He and his followers headed north in November of 1861, pursued by hostile Creeks under the command of a colonel from Texas named Douglas Cooper. Clashes with Cooper's warriors and the travails of the journey deprived the fugitives of most of their possessions. Their leader died sometime after they arrived in Kansas. Utterly dependent on the federal government, the Creeks lived there for nearly three years in a dismal tent city.

The Cherokee were even more bitterly divided by the war. For a time, John Ross tried to hold the nation together. Although he had little enthusiasm for the Confederate cause, he knew that Stand Watie and other prominent Cherokee slaveholders were deeply committed to it, and he agreed to sign a treaty with the Confederates in August of 1861. He could not compel all of his followers to go along with his decision, however. Later that year, Cherokee warriors were asked to join in Colonel Cooper's pursuit of the Creeks led by Opothle Yoholo. Rather than attack other Indi-

Arbors representing the seven Cherokee clans ring a fireplace at an Oklahoma site for the Stomp Dance. During the dance, smoke from a sacred flame in the fireplace carries prayers skyward to the spirits above.

Keetoowah Society leader Red Bird Smith (second from left) and other prominent members display the group's seven sacred wampum belts in a 1916 photograph. Created in the 1700s from bits of shell strung onto twine, the belts have religious messages encoded in their designs.

KEEPERS OF THE FLAME

Amid the cultural and political turmoil that plagued the southern tribes during the second half of the 19th century, a Cherokee group known as the Keetoowah Society managed to create an oasis of order for its nation by reviving traditions that had withered after the move west. According to Cherokee legend, the group takes its name from Kituhwa, the northernmost town of the ancient Cherokee Nation in the East. The town's geographic position meant that its people shouldered the task of defending the entire nation from invading northern tribes. When Englishmen pushed into Cherokee territory, the townsmen of Kituhwa fought them as well, rejecting European ways.

After the Cherokee emigrated to the Indian Territory, Kituhwa no longer existed as a distinct place, but some Western Cherokees still held tightly to Kituhwa convictions. In 1859 these individuals organized themselves into the Keetoowah Society, a political group whose more radical members eventually advocated violence against whites. Over the span of the next two decades, however, the Keetoowahs evolved into a peaceful religious society devoted to revitalizing a disintegrating culture by restoring old ceremonies and rituals, such as the Green Corn Ceremony and the Stomp Dance.

Today, Keetoowah Society members continue to keep ancient traditions alive, and the group itself has become so central to the preservation of tribal life that it has been called the "religious arm of the Cherokee Nation."

Members of the Bird Clan perform the White Feather Dance, part of the Green Corn Ceremony that is still held each summer to usher in the new year. The ritual is one of many revived by the Keetoowahs.

In front of an Oklahoma courthouse in 1892, the lifeless arms of Ned Christie cradle a rifle. A Keetoowah radical who waged a violent war against whites, Christie was killed in a shootout with federal marshals.

Fashioned from a box turtle shell filled with pebbles, this rattle was formerly used by a dance leader to summon participants in the Stomp Dance. Rattles made from dried gourds are a modern substitute.

This rare photograph, taken with a video camera at night and published here for the first time, shows modern stomp dancers in Oklahoma singing and dancing around the sacred fire. The springtime ritual renews the community's ties with the Great Spirit and launches a cycle of ceremonies.

To provide rhythm for the Stomp Dance and accompaniment for the singing, women dancers traditionally wore leg rattles made from pebble-filled turtle shells (below). Modern rattles are sometimes made from milk cans (right).

Modern leaders of the Keetoowah Society hold up the sacred wampum belts passed on to them by their ancestors. Each year the meaning of the belts is retold in a ceremony held shortly after the Stomp Dance.

ans, an entire regiment of Cherokee traditionalists opposed to the slave-holders renounced the Confederate cause and fled from Cooper's camp.

In 1862 federal forces invaded Cherokee territory. John Ross gladly abandoned his support for the Confederacy and traveled east. But Stand Watie held out, declaring himself principal chief of the nation and claiming the power to conscript Cherokees for Confederate service. An able commander, he eventually rose to the rank of brigadier general. Tragically, his soldiers often found themselves pitted against Unionist Cherokees—known as Pins for an insignia they wore. Among those affected by the strife was Hannah Hicks, the daughter of missionary Samuel Worcester and the wife of a Cherokee Unionist. She saw her husband killed by Pins, who mistook him for a Confederate, and her house sacked by Stand Watie's men. "Alas, alas, for this miserable people," she lamented, "destroying each other as fast as they can."

Although the Cherokee paid an especially steep toll during the war, no group in the Indian Territory escaped devastation as opposing forces swept back and forth, burning and pilfering. When peace came at last in 1865, many Indians were as destitute as the survivors of the Trail of Tears some 30 years earlier.

For the people of the Indian Territory as for the vanquished Confederates, the Union victory brought an end to slavery. The Cherokee alone emancipated 4,000 slaves, who were entitled by treaty to citizenship in the Cherokee Nation and allotments of land—although some of those freed were discriminated against and later emigrated. Emancipation was

Followers of the Creek traditionalist Chitto Harjo, or Crazy Snake, assemble inside the federal prison at Fort Gibson in 1901 after their arrest for menacing so-called progressive Indians. As defenders of the old ways, Crazy Snake and his supporters opposed individual land allotments, renting land to whites, and the use of white labor.

Deeds like the one shown at right, belonging to Cherokee Robert P. Vann, were used to verify title to individually owned parcels of land after the U.S. Congress passed legislation authorizing the breakup of tribal holdings.

inevitable, but other measures imposed by the federal government after the war were arbitrary and exploitive. Ignoring the fact that many Indians had supported the Union, the federal government used treaties the tribes had signed with the Confederacy as grounds for requiring them to grant rights of way to the railroads and cede huge chunks of land, much of which went to provide reservations for Plains tribes that were being removed from areas coveted by white ranchers, settlers, or miners. Altogether, members of 62 other tribes were eventually transplanted to share the Indian Territory with the original occupants.

Once again the five tribes worked for a generation to rebuild their institutions, only to be undermined by outside forces. In 1887 Congress passed the General Allotment, or Dawes, Act, which provided for private ownership of land by American Indians. Small tracts would be allotted to individual families, and the remaining lands would then be sold to white settlers, with the proceeds to be divided up among members of the tribe. Supporters of the act argued that allotment, by ending tribal ownership and undercutting tribal government, would further the assimilation of Indians into white society. The people of the Five Nations—as they regarded themselves—yearned to remain distinct, and they managed to obtain exemptions from the allotment act. Within a few years, however, Congress yielded to pressure from whites who had already infiltrated the Indian Territory and imposed on the Indians both an allotment program and U.S. citizenship—a dubious privilege for people who proudly claimed citizenship in their own nations.

Allotment forced Indians to part with land for as little as $1.40 per acre. What remained to them was often inadequate for a family to prosper on, given the limited productivity of the soil. A Cherokee named DeWitt Clinton Duncan, who had graduated from Dartmouth College in 1861 and later served as a teacher and tribal leader, found himself at the age of 76 attempting to eke out a living on an allotment of 60 acres. "Under the old Cherokee regime, I spent the early days of my life on the farm up here of 300 acres and arranged to be comfortable in my old age," he testified before a Senate committee. "But the allotment scheme came along and struck

THE CHOCTAW FAIR

Each summer the traditional spirit of the Choctaw Nation comes alive on the Pearl River Reservation at Philadelphia, Mississippi, when descendants of Choctaws who refused to be removed from their ancestral homeland hold an annual fair. Just as the tribe used to assemble to honor the ripening of the year's first corn, Choctaws from all across the country travel to Pearl River to share in this celebration of their common cultural heritage. Begun in 1949, four years after the reservation in Mississippi was established, the four-day festival has become a popular tourist attraction, featuring traditional Choctaw dances, storytelling, handicrafts, and the world series of ishtaboli, the traditional Choctaw ball game.

A couple hold hands as they perform the Friendship Dance. Although the style of their clothing is nontraditional, the colorful needlework and necklaces are pure Choctaw.

A wavy line of performers coils and uncoils during the Snake Dance. Birds and animals were paramount in the lives of the ancient Choctaws, who honored the creatures with special dances.

The Choctaw Fair has activities for every generation. The 16-year-old girl at far left was the winner of the Choctaw Indian Princess contest; the elder at left served as a chanter, the person responsible for setting the beat for certain dances.

Members of the winning team in the 1993 Ishtaboli World Series proudly display their trophy. There is also a championship in a youth division for boys ages 11 to 14.

Master basket maker Eleanor Ferris demonstrates her craft. A skilled practitioner can weave a Choctaw basket of swamp cane in about one week, including the time spent splitting, stripping, and dyeing the cane.

me during the crop season, while my corn was ripening in full ear." Reduced to a plot one-fifth the size of his original holding, he found himself mired in debt. "For the last few years, since I have had my allotment, I have gone out there on that farm day after day," he added. "I have used the ax, the hoe, the spade, the plow, hour for hour, until fatigue would throw me exhausted upon the ground. Next day I repeated the operation, and let me tell you, Senators, I have exerted all my ability, all industry, all my intelligence, if I have any, my will, my ambition, the love of my wife—all these agencies I have employed to make a living out of that 60 acres, and, God be my judge, I have not been able to do it."

Duncan's compelling testimony, delivered in 1906, came at a time when native occupants of the Indian Territory were waging a last-ditch battle to avoid being absorbed by the proposed state of Oklahoma. By now, white settlers had already transformed the western portion of the Indian Territory into the Oklahoma Territory. To preserve what was left to them, leaders of the Five Nations had drafted a constitution for their own state, named after Sequoya, inventor of the Cherokee alphabet. Congress ignored their proposal and subsumed the remaining Indian Territory within the state of Oklahoma, which was admitted to the Union in 1907. Ironically, the state's very name was Indian, derived from the Choctaw words *okla* (people) and *homma* (red).

Creeks, Choctaws, Chickasaws, Cherokees, and Seminoles were now residents of Oklahoma. But they would not surrender their identities. Through the 20th century, they preserved distinct communities across the state and retained their ancestral languages, values, and customs. Today many still celebrate a version of the Green Corn Ceremony to renew their spirits, recite the old stories and songs, and play a form of the traditional stickball game. To help preserve their rights and traditions, all five groups maintain councils with elected representatives. And in recent years, the people of the West have renewed ties with the descendants of the people who stayed behind in the east—whether on reservations like those of the Choctaws in Mississippi or the Seminoles in Florida, or in independent settlements like those of the Cherokees in western North Carolina.

Today, more than a century and a half after the ordeal of removal, Indians frequently travel hundreds of miles back and forth between Oklahoma and the southeastern states to celebrate their common heritage. Once a source of sorrow, the journey has become an occasion for hope, as native southerners come together to rekindle the proud fires that once burned in the heart of every Indian town. ❖

Practicing the wisdom of the past, Peter Dyer, a Mississippi Choctaw medicine man, turns his face to the sky during a rainmaking ritual. Dyer is an "apoluma," one of three types of Choctaw conjurers, whose powers included the ability to bring rain, predict future events, ensure success at hunting, impart bravery to warriors, and treat illnesses.

BOUNTY FROM MOTHER CORN

Since ancient times, the Indians of the southern woodlands have cherished corn as a life-sustaining gift from the spirits. Although the traditional fare of the region's tribes included such items as venison, fish, beans, and squash, it was corn that filled the storehouses and provided for villagers through the year. The plant became an object of wonder and veneration as well as a culinary staple. In the words of the Cherokee people, "Maize was our life."

Today members of the tribes that once dominated the South depend far less on corn than their ancestors did, but the ancient cycle of planting and harvesting still governs the spiritual and cultural rhythms of many communities. Legends endure of the sacred corn mother who gave of her body to nourish future generations.

Such bounty sustained not only the original southerners but also the Europeans who encountered them. Some early white settlers were driven to the brink of starvation when crops they brought with them from the Old World failed; they thrived when they learned to plant maize and prepare it much as the Indians did. From this adaptive process came dishes that are recognized today as distinctive southern delicacies.

A tattooed Indian woman offers fresh ears of corn to her guests in a 16th-century drawing by an English colonist along the Carolina coast. Women cultivated and cooked the grain, although men helped clear and prepare the fields.

This 1542 woodcut was one of the first printed illustrations of corn, a plant foreign to Europe. One Italian visitor to the New World reported that grinding the corn produces a fine flour: "A bread of excellent flavor is made from it."

In a modern depiction of an ancient legend, corn sprouts from the body of Selu, who has been slain by her two club-wielding sons. Curious as to where their mother got her corn, the boys spied on her and found that the kernels came from her body. At Selu's bidding, the boys killed her and used her remains to consecrate the first cornfield. Today the Cherokee revere her as Mother Corn.

Men turn the soil with bone-tipped hoes while women plant corn in holes dug with a stick in this 1564 engraving of an Indian village. The furrows are a fanciful touch by the European artist.

EXPLOITING THE HARVEST

Wielding simple tools made from wood, stone, shell, and bone, the woodlands Indians evolved efficient methods for cultivating and processing corn. They planted the seed corn in May; instead of broadcasting kernels over furrows, they inserted them in mounds of earth. These hillocks held fast in heavy rains that would have washed away the soil had the ground been gouged by plows.

Dried in the husk and placed in storehouses in the fall, corn was prepared for consumption as needed. After shelling the corn, women soaked it in lye made from a solution of ashes and water to loosen the thick hull encasing each kernel. The hulled corn was then ground to produce meal, which could be moistened and baked to yield cakes or bread or boiled to produce a nutritious gruel.

Some women in the southern woodlands ground corn by spreading the hulled kernels over a large stone (bottom) and pounding them into meal with a smaller hand-held stone.

In a 16th-century engraving, Indians in a dugout paddle a load of corn and other crops to the village storehouse (background). Crops were raised communally and shared by all in the Southeast.

Women perched on scaffolds serve as scarecrows by shooing hungry birds away from a cornfield in this 19th-century portrait of a practice common among Indians from the Great Lakes to the Deep South. Observed one visitor to Cherokee country, "This usually is the duty of old women, who fret at the very shadow of a crow."

Two Seminole women grind corn about 1940 using a mortar and pestles similar to the wooden implements displayed (inset). Although this traditional technique was less efficient than the water-powered gristmills that were common in Indian communities by the late 1800s, women enjoyed the ceremony and companionship that went with hand grinding, and some continued to make their cornmeal the old-fashioned way.

A PRODUCTIVE EXCHANGE

Some early European settlers viewed corn with disdain. Complained one Englishman, "It nourisheth but little and is a more convenient food for swine than for man." When Old World crops such as wheat wilted in the hot southern sun, however, whites turned in desperation to the strange New World grain, learning from Indians how to plant and cultivate it.

In return, the immigrants introduced the Indians to worthy new tools and techniques. Iron-bladed hoes and hatchets, for example, proved far more efficient for clearing fields and weeding crops than traditional implements tipped with stone or bone. And carting corn to the local mill was often easier than grinding it by hand. But not all Indian farmers embraced such innovations. Many adhered to ancestral practices well into the 20th century.

The Mingus Creek Mill, pictured here in 1937, served the Cherokees who held out in western North Carolina after most members of the tribe were removed to Oklahoma. Such mills became obsolete in the 20th century as Indian women turned to packaged cornmeal.

Three items traded to Creeks by 17th-century Spaniards— an iron axhead (below, left), a hoe blade (center), and an adz—typify the European hardware that replaced Indian tools. Among the native devices that endured were basket sifters (left), used to separate loose hulls.

Florida Indians prepare a feast in this 16th-century engraving. At center, one man pours ground corn into a pot of boiling water.

At a Cherokee social gathering about 1930, pots of corn broth are among the dishes awaiting the hungry guests.

Carved about 1900, this spoon is typical of those long used by Creeks and kindred Seminoles to feast on sofke.

A YEN FOR FEASTING

In recent times, Native Americans who trace their origins to the southern woodlands have lost touch with some of their traditions, but they remain as attached as ever to corn and the large number of wholesome dishes derived from it. Events such as weddings, graduations, and county fairs would scarcely be complete without time-honored delicacies such as corn bread and the zesty corn broth that Creeks season with a dash of lye and call "sofke."

Corn remains an essential accompaniment not only for worldly celebrations but also for rituals of praise and thanksgiving. Even where the crop is no longer grown, the season in which the ears ripen—midsummer—retains special significance. Traditionally, this was the time for the Green Corn Ceremony—the celebration of the beginning of a new year—and many Indians still mark the joyous transition by cleaning out homes, declaring an end to old animosities, and savoring the first fruits of the harvest. Whatever the occasion, native peoples from Oklahoma to Florida prize the gifts of Mother Corn as food for the spirit as well as the body.

*Preparing for a
gathering with her
fellow Creeks at a
church near Okmul-
gee, Oklahoma,
Pauline Billy ladles
out sofke (below)—
the perfect accom-
paniment to a slice
of sour corn bread
(left). According to
legend, sofke
was heaven sent,
having spilled down
to earth through a
tear in the sky.*

THE FLAVORFUL LEGACY

Today Indian cuisine is consumed by Americans everywhere, although most people are unaware of its origins. Southern cooking in particular owes much to the Indians. From them colonists learned to prepare pone, a crisp bread made by mixing cornmeal and water and frying the dough on a hot griddle or stone; a similar process yielded the nuggets of fried corn dough called hush puppies. By adding milk or eggs and baking the dough, European Americans came up with a fluffy type of pone known as corn bread. The regional specialty called grits, however, has changed little since Indians began mixing a coarse type of cornmeal—known today by the Algonquian term hominy—with enough hot water to produce a thick, granular porridge. The seasonings for this dish may vary: Indians traditionally mixed in some bear grease or other animal fat, while many people now prefer butter. But whatever the accompaniment, southerners relish grits as soul-soothing fare.

Among the popular dishes inspired by recipes Indians devised for cornmeal (above, left) are corn bread (foreground) and the fried treats pone and hush puppies (center) along with the venerable grits (above, right).

ACKNOWLEDGMENTS

The editors wish to thank the following for their valuable assistance in the preparation of this book:

In England:
London—Jim Hamill

In Germany:
Berlin—Peter Bolz, Staatliche Museen zu Berlin-Preussischer Kulturbesitz, Museum für Völkerkunde; Heidi Klein, Bildarchiv Preussischer Kulturbesitz.

In the United States:
Maryland: Adelphi—Valerie Wooldridge.
Nebraska: Chadron—Charles Hanson, Jr., Museum of the Fur Trade.
North Carolina: Cherokee—Margie Douthit, Cherokee Historical Association; Betty DuPree, Qualla Arts and Crafts Center; Joanne Greene, Museum of the Cherokee Indian.
Oklahoma: Fort Sill—Towana Spivey, Fort Sill Museum. Muskogee—Thomas R. McKinney, Bacone College Museum; Lynn Thornley, Five Civilized Tribes Museum. Norman—Julie Droke, Oklahoma Museum of Natural History; John R. Lovett, Western History Collections, University of Oklahoma Library. Oklahoma City—Oklahoma Historical Society. Tahlequah—Carol J. Dunn, Tom Mooney, Cherokee National Historical Society, Inc.; Murv Jacob; Sammy Still, Cherokee Nation. Tulsa—William Donahue, Greg Easterley, Johnny Thomason, KJRH, Channel 2. Wewoka—Willie Lena; Jan Wyrick, The Seminole Nation Museum.
Virginia: Alexandria—Ann V. Kelly.

BIBLIOGRAPHY

America's Fascinating Indian Heritage. Pleasantville, New York: Reader's Digest Association, 1978.

Anderson, William L., ed., *Cherokee Removal: Before and After.* Athens: University of Georgia Press, 1991.

Bancroft-Hunt, Norman, *North American Indians.* Philadelphia: Courage Books, 1992.

Bodmer, Karl, *Karl Bodmer's America.* Omaha: University of Nebraska Press, 1984.

Brain, Jeffrey P., *The Tunica-Biloxi.* New York: Chelsea House Publishers, 1990.

Braund, Kathryn E. Holland, *Deerskins & Duffels: The Creek Indian Trade with Anglo-America, 1685-1815.* Lincoln: University of Nebraska Press, 1993.

Bridges, Marilyn, *Markings: Aerial Views of Sacred Landscapes.* New York: Aperture Foundation, 1986.

Brown, Calvin S., *Archeology of Mississippi.* University: Mississippi Geological Survey, 1926.

Casagrande, Joseph B., ed., *In the Company of Man: Twenty Portraits by Anthropologists.* New York: Harper & Brothers, 1960.

Collins, Richard, ed., *The Native Americans: The Indigenous People of North America.* New York: Smithmark Publications, 1991.

Corkran, David H., *The Creek Frontier: 1540-1783.* Norman: University of Oklahoma Press, 1967.

Cotterill, R. S., *The Southern Indians: The Story of the Civilized Tribes before Removal.* Norman: University of Oklahoma Press, 1954.

Cox, Beverly, and Martin Jacobs, *Spirit of the Harvest: North American Indian Cooking.* New York: Stewart, Tabori & Chang, 1991.

Crane, Verner W., *The Southern Frontier: 1670-1732.* Ann Arbor: University of Michigan Press, 1956 (reprint of 1929 edition).

Crumrine, N. Ross, and Marjorie Halpin, eds., *The Power of Symbols: Masks and Masquerade in the Americas.* Vancouver: University of British Columbia Press, 1983.

Debo, Angie, *And Still the Waters Run: The Betrayal of the Five Civilized Tribes.* Princeton: Princeton University Press, 1972.

DeRosier, Arthur H., Jr., *The Removal of the Choctaw Indians.* Knoxville: University of Tennessee Press, 1970.

De Vorsey, Louis, Jr., ed., *De Brahm's Report of the General Survey in the Southern District of North America.* Columbia: University of South Carolina Press, 1971.

Dillon, Richard H., *North American Indian Wars.* New York: Gallery Books, 1983.

Dye, David H., and Cheryl Anne Cox, eds., *Towns and Temples along the Mississippi.* Tuscaloosa: University of Alabama Press, 1990.

Ehle, John, *Trail of Tears: The Rise and Fall of the Cherokee Nation.* New York: Anchor Books, 1989.

Fogelson, Raymond D., *The Cherokees: A Critical Bibliography.* Bloomington: Indiana University 1978.

Fogelson, Raymond D., and Amelia R. Bell, "Cherokee Booger Mask Tradition," in *The Power of Symbols: Masks and Masquerade in the Americas.* Vancouver: University of British Columbia Press, 1983.

Foreman, Grant:
The Five Civilized Tribes: Cherokee, Chickasaw, Choctaw, Creek, Seminole. Norman: University of Oklahoma Press, 1934.
Indian Removal: The Emigration of the Five Civilized Tribes of Indians. Norman: University of Oklahoma Press, 1972.
Sequoyah. Norman: University of Oklahoma Press, 1938.

Fundaburk, Emma Lila, ed., *Southeastern Indians Life Portraits: A Catalogue of Pictures, 1564-1860.* Luverne, Alabama: Emma Lila Fundaburk, 1958.

Garbarino, Merwyn S., *The Seminole.* New York: Chelsea House Publishers, 1989.

Gibson, Arrell M., *The Chickasaws.* Norman: University of Oklahoma Press, 1971.

Gibson, Arrell Morgan, ed., *America's Exiles: Indian Colonization in Oklahoma.* Oklahoma City: Oklahoma Historical Society, 1976.

Giles, Dorothy, *Singing Valleys: The Story of Corn.* New York: Random House, 1940.

Green, Donald E., *The Creek People.* Phoenix: Indian Tribal Series, 1973.

Green, Michael D.:
The Creeks. New York: Chelsea House Publishers, 1990.
The Creeks: A Critical Bibliography. Bloomington: Indiana University Press, 1979.

Hale, Duane K., and Arrell M. Gibson, *The Chickasaw.* New York: Chelsea House Publishers, 1991.

Hartley, William, and Ellen Hartley, *Osceola: The Unconquered Indian.* New York: Hawthorn Books, 1973.

Hassrick, Royal B., *The George Catlin Book of American Indians.* New York: Promontory Press, 1988.

Hendrix, Janey B., *Redbird Smith and the Nighthawk Keetoowahs.* Park Hill, Oklahoma: Cross-Cultural Education Center, 1984.

Highwater, Jamake, *Ritual of the Wind: North American Indian Ceremonies, Music, and Dance.* Toronto: Methuen Publications, 1984.

Howard, James H., *Oklahoma Seminoles: Medicines, Magic, and Religion.* Norman: University of Oklahoma Press, 1984.

Howard, James H., and Victoria Lindsay Levine, *Choctaw Music and Dance.* Norman: University of Oklahoma Press, 1990.

Hudson, Charles, *The Southeastern Indians.* Knoxville: University of Tennessee Press, 1976.

Hudson, Charles M., ed., *Four Centuries of Southern Indians.* Athens: University of Georgia Press, 1975.

Jahoda, Gloria, *The Trail of Tears.* New York: Holt, Rinehart and Winston, 1975.

Josephy, Alvin M., Jr., ed., *The American Heritage Book of Indians.* New York: American Heritage Publishing, 1961.

Kidwell, Clara Sue, and Charles Roberts, *The Choctaws: A Critical Bibliography.* Bloomington: Indiana University Press, 1980.

Kilpatrick, Jack Frederick, *Sequoyah: Of Earth and Intellect.* Austin: Encino Press, 1965.

Lawson, John, *A New Voyage to Carolina.* Ed. by Hugh Talmage Lefler. Chapel Hill: University of North Carolina Press, 1967.

Lewis, Thomas M. N., and Madeline Kneberg Lewis:
Eva: An Archaic Site. Knoxville: University of Tennessee Press, 1961.
Hiwassee Island: An Archaeological Account of Four Tennessee Indian Peoples. Knoxville: University of Tennessee Press, 1946.
Tribes That Slumber: Indian Times in the Tennessee Region. Knoxville: University of Tennessee Press, 1958.
Lieut. Henry Timberlake's Memoirs: 1756-1765. Marietta, Georgia: Continental Book Company, 1948.

Lumpkin, Henry, *From Savannah to Yorktown: The American Revolution in the South.* Columbia: University of South Carolina Press, 1981.

Mahon, John K., *History of the Second Seminole War, 1835-1842.* Gainesville: University of Florida Press, 1967.

Mails, Thomas E., *The Cherokee People: The Story of the Cherokees from Earliest Origins to Contemporary Times.* Tulsa, Oklahoma: Council Oak Books, 1992.

Mancini, Richard E., *Indians of the Southeast.* New York: Facts On File, 1992.

Mangelsdorf, Paul C., *Corn: Its Origin, Evolution and Improvement.* Cambridge: Belknap Press of Harvard University Press, 1974.

Martin, Joel W., *Sacred Revolt: The Muskogees' Struggle for a New World.* Boston: Beacon Press, 1991.

McKee, Jesse O., *The Choctaw.* New York: Chelsea House Publishers, 1989.

McKee, Jesse O., and Jon A. Schlenker, *The Choctaws: Cultural Evolution of a Native American Tribe.* Jackson: University Press of Mississippi, 1980.

Merrell, James H., *The Indians' New World: Catawbas and Their Neighbors from European Contact through the Era of Removal.* Chapel Hill: University of North Carolina Press, 1989.

Moore, Alexander, ed., *Nairne's Muskhogean Journals: The 1708 Expedition to the Mississippi River.* Jackson: University Press of Mississippi, 1988.

Moulton, Gary E., *John Ross: Cherokee Chief.* Athens: University of Georgia Press, 1978.

Moulton, Gary E., ed., *The Papers of Chief John Ross* (2 vols.). Norman: University of Oklahoma Press, 1985.

Nabokov, Peter, ed., *Native American Testimony.* New York: Penguin Books, 1991.

Nabokov, Peter, and Robert Easton, *Native American Architecture.* New York: Oxford University Press, 1989.

Perdue, Theda:

The Cherokee. New York: Chelsea House Publishers, 1989.

Nations Remembered: An Oral History of the Five Civilized Tribes, 1865-1907. Westport, Connecticut: Greenwood Press, 1980.

Slavery and the Evolution of Cherokee Society: 1540-1866. Knoxville: University of Tennessee Press, 1979.

Peterson, John H., Jr., ed., *A Choctaw Source Book.* New York: Garland Publishing, 1985.

Randolph, F. Ralph, *British Travelers among the Southern Indians, 1660-1763.* Norman: University of Oklahoma Press, 1973.

Reeves, Carolyn Keller, ed., *The Choctaw before Removal.* Jackson: University Press of Mississippi, 1985.

Reid, John Phillip, *A Better Kind of Hatchet: Law, Trade, and Diplomacy in the Cherokee Nation during the Early Years of European Contact.* University Park: Pennsylvania State University Press, 1976.

Rights, Douglas L., *The American Indian in North Carolina.* Winston-Salem, North Carolina: John F. Blair, 1957.

Shaffer, Lynda Norene, *Native Americans before 1492: The Moundbuilding Centers of the Eastern Woodlands.* Armonk, New York: M. E. Sharpe, 1992.

Sharpe, J. Ed, and Thomas B. Underwood, *American Indian Cooking & Herb Lore.* Cherokee, North Carolina: Cherokee Publications, 1973.

Speck, Frank G., and Leonard Broom, *Cherokee Dance and Drama.* Berkeley: University of California Press, 1951.

Sturtevant, William C., ed., *A Seminole Source Book.* New York: Garland Publishing, 1987.

Swanton, John R., *The Indians of the Southeastern United States.* Washington, D.C.: Smithsonian Institution Press, 1979.

Underwood, Thomas Bryan, *The Story of the Cherokee People.* Cherokee, North Carolina: Cherokee Publications, 1961.

Wallace, Anthony F. C., *The Long, Bitter Trail: Andrew Jackson and the Indians.* New York: Hill and Wang, 1993.

Weatherford, Jack, *Indian Givers: How the Indians of the Americas Transformed the World.* New York: Crown Publishers, 1988.

Weatherwax, Paul, *Indian Corn in Old America.* New York: MacMillan Company, 1954.

Welch, Paul D., *Moundville's Economy.* Tuscaloosa: University of Alabama Press, 1991.

Wells, Samuel J., and Roseanna Tubby, eds., *After Removal: The Choctaw in Mississippi.* Jackson: University Press of Mississippi, 1986.

Wickman, Patricia R., *Osceola's Legacy.* Tuscaloosa: University of Alabama Press, 1991.

Wilkins, Thurman, *Cherokee Tragedy: The Ridge Family and the Decimation of a People.* Norman: University of Oklahoma Press, 1986.

Williams, Samuel Cole, ed., *Adair's History of the American Indians.* Johnson City, Tennessee: Watauga Press, 1930.

Wood, Peter H., Gregory A. Waselkov, and M. Thomas Hatley, eds., *Powhatan's Mantle: Indians in the Colonial Southeast.* Lincoln: University of Nebraska Press, 1989.

Wright, J. Leitch, Jr.:

Creeks & Seminoles: The Destruction and Regeneration of the Muscogulge People. Lincoln: University of Nebraska Press, 1986.

The Only Land They Knew: The Tragic Story of the American Indians in the Old South. New York: Free Press, 1981.

PERIODICALS

Fogelson, Raymond D., "The Conjuror in Eastern Cherokee Society." *Journal of Cherokee Studies,* Fall 1980.

Fogelson, Raymond D., and Amelia B. Walker, "Self and Other in Cherokee Booger Masks." *Journal of Cherokee Studies,* Fall 1980.

Greene, Joan, and H. F. Robinson, "Maize Was Our Life: A History of Cherokee Corn." *Journal of Cherokee Studies,* Spring 1986.

Greenlee, Robert F., "Medicine and Curing Practices of the Modern Florida Seminoles." *American Anthropologist,* July-September 1944.

Haas, Mary R., "Creek Inter-Town Relations." *American Anthropologist,* July-September 1940.

Hanson, Charles E., Jr., "The Southern Fur Trade: A Slightly Different Story." *The Museum of the Fur Trade Quarterly,* Spring 1986.

Hendrix, Janey B., "Redbird Smith and the Nighthawk Keetoowahs." *Journal of Cherokee Studies,* Spring 1983.

Kelsey, Julie, ed., *The Choctaw Community News,* July 1993.

McCoy, Ronald, "Mother Corn: Native America's Legendary Staff of Life." *The World & I,* November 1991.

Sturtevant, William C.:

"The Medicine Bundles and Busks of the Florida Seminole." *The Florida Anthropologist,* May 1954.

"Osceola's Coats?" *The Florida Historical Quarterly,* April 1956.

OTHER PUBLICATIONS

Chapman, Jefferson, "Tellico Archaeology: 12,000 Years of Native American History." Publications in Anthropology No. 41. Knoxville: Tennessee Valley Authority, 1985.

Geiger, Maynard, "The Franciscan Conquest of Florida: 1573-1618." Doctoral dissertation. Washington, D.C.: Catholic University of America, 1937.

King, Duane H., *Cherokee Heritage: Official Guidebook to the Museum of the Cherokee Indian.* Cherokee, North Carolina: Museum of the Cherokee Indian, 1988.

Persistence of Pattern In Mississippi Choctaw Culture. Catalog. Jackson: Mississippi Department of Archives and History, 1987.

PICTURE CREDITS

The sources for the illustrations that appear in this book are listed below. Credits from left to right are separated by semicolons; from top to bottom they are separated by dashes.

Cover: © Gene Boaz. **6-15:** Border art by Time-Life Books. Photographs © Marilyn Bridges. **16:** Gilcrease Museum, Tulsa, Oklahoma, accession no. 0176.1015. **20:** Copyright British Museum, London. **21:** David H. Dye, courtesy Memphis State University, Chucalissa Site Anthropology Department, Tennessee. **23:** © John Elk III. **24:** Map by Maryland CartoGraphics, Inc. **25:** Courtesy Chickasaw Nation, Ada, Oklahoma, photographed by Rod Wellington. **27:** University of Mississippi, Calvin Brown Collection. **28, 29:** National Anthropological Archives, NAA, Smithsonian Institution, nos. 45838-H; 1159-9; 1071-A. **30:** NAA, Smithsonian Institution, no. 1007; Western History Collections, University of Oklahoma Library. **31:** Courtesy Mississippi Department of Archives and History; NAA, Smithsonian Institution, no. 1011. **32, 33:** NAA, Smithsonian Institution, nos. 45836; 1024; 56537. **34-37:** Art by Bobbi Tull. **38, 39:** Art by Bobbi Tull, insets courtesy Oconaluftee Indian Village, a reconstructed 1750 village, Cherokee, North Carolina, photographed by Ron Ruel. **40:** Western History Collections, University of Oklahoma Library—Oklahoma State Museum of History. **42:** Stephanie B. Berryhill, courtesy Muscogee (Creek) Nation Communications Department, Okmulgee, Oklahoma. **43:** © Carole Thompson. **44:** Courtesy Saint Louis Science Center, Saint Louis, Missouri. **45:** Courtesy The Seminole Nation Museum, Wewoka, Oklahoma, photographed by Steve Tuttle. **46, 47:** Staatliche Museen zu Berlin-Preussischer Kulturbesitz, Kunstbibliothek. **48, 49:** NAA, Smithsonian Institution, nos. 45,489-B; 1178-N-8-1. **50, 51:** Courtesy Cherokee Historical Association, Cherokee, North Carolina; courtesy Cherokee Heritage Center, Tahlequah, Oklahoma (3); Peter T. Furst. **52:** National Gallery of Art, Washington, D.C. **55:** Smithsonian Institution, no. 13249. **56, 57:** Courtesy The Seminole Nation Museum, Wewoka, Oklahoma, photographed by Steve Tuttle. **58, 59:** Drawings by Willie Lena, from *Oklahoma Seminoles: Medicine, Magic, and Religion* by James H. Howard, University of Oklahoma Press, Norman, 1984 (2)—courtesy The Seminole Nation Museum, Wewoka, Oklahoma, photographed by Steve Tuttle (2); drawing by Willie Lena, courtesy The Seminole Nation Museum, Wewoka, Oklahoma, photographed by Steve Tuttle. **60-65:** Drawings by Willie Lena, from *Oklahoma Seminoles: Medicine, Magic, and Religion* by James H. Howard, University of Oklahoma Press, Norman, 1984, artifacts courtesy The Seminole Nation Museum, Wewoka, Oklahoma, photographed by Steve Tuttle. **66:** The National Museum of Den-

mark, Department of Ethnography, Copenhagen—NAA, Smithsonian Institution, no. 1063-H-I. **68, 69:** Burgerbibliothek, Bern, Switzerland. **72, 73:** Copyright British Museum, London. **74:** Royal Library, Copenhagen. **75:** NAA, Smithsonian Institution, no. 1102-B-26—Staatliche Museen zu Berlin-Preussischer Kulturbesitz, Museum für Völkerkunde, foto Dietrich Graf. **77:** NAA, Smithsonian Institution, no. 44039. **78-83:** Museum of the Fur Trade, Chadron, Nebraska. **85:** The National Museum of Denmark, Department of Ethnography, Copenhagen. **86, 87:** Jennie Elrod Collection, Oklahoma Historical Society (3); top right, courtesy Oconaluftee Indian Village, a reconstructed 1750 village, Cherokee, North Carolina, photographed by Ron Ruel—bottom left, courtesy Five Civilized Tribes Museum, Muskogee, Oklahoma, photographed by Steve Tuttle. **89:** Map by Maryland CartoGraphics, Inc. **90:** Courtesy Public Record Office, London (Map C0700 Carolina 21). **91:** The Granger Collection, New York. **92, 93:** Painting by Murv Jacob, Tahlequah, Oklahoma. **94, 95:** The National Museum of Denmark, Department of Ethnography, Copenhagen, photographs by Kit Weiss. **96:** Courtesy Qualla Arts & Crafts Mutual, Inc., Cherokee, North Carolina, photographed by Scott Dobbins. **97:** The National Museum of Denmark, Department of Ethnography, Copenhagen. **98:** NAA, Smithsonian Institution, no. 1000-A. **100, 101:** Map by Maryland CartoGraphics, Inc.; Woolaroc Museum, Bartlesville, Oklahoma—courtesy Five Civilized Tribes Museum, Muskogee, Oklahoma, photographed by Steve Tuttle. **102, 103:** © David Lawrence/Panoramic Images—© Jonathan Wallen; Missouri Department of Natural Resources, Division of State Parks, photographed by Greg Henson. **104, 105:** Gilcrease Museum, Tulsa, Oklahoma, accession no. 0227.1487; © Gene Boaz. **106, 107:** © Gene Boaz (2); Missouri Department of Natural Resources, Division of State Parks, photographed by Greg Henson. **108, 109:** Missouri Department of Natural Resources, Division of State Parks, photographed by Greg Henson—painting by Murv Jacob, Tahlequah, Oklahoma. **110, 111:** © John Elk III (2)—National Museum of American Art, Washington, D.C./Art Resource, New York. **112:** Western History Collections, University of Oklahoma Library. **115:** Alabama Department of Archives and History, photographed by John E. Scott, Jr. **118, 119:** Map by Maryland CartoGraphics, Inc. **120, 121:** Courtesy Five Civilized Tribes Museum, Muskogee, Oklahoma, photographed by Steve Tuttle. **122:** Woolaroc Museum, Bartlesville, Oklahoma—Western History Collections, University of Oklahoma Library. **123:** Neg. no. 124781, courtesy Department of Library Services, American Museum of Natural History—NAA, Smithsonian Institution, no. 1063-L—Western History Collections, University of Oklahoma Library. **127-130:** National Museum of American Art, Washington, D.C./Art

Resource, New York. **133:** Clements Library, University of Michigan. **134, 135:** Joslyn Art Museum, Omaha, Nebraska, gift of Enron Art Foundation. **136, 137:** The Philbrook Museum of Art, Tulsa, Oklahoma; Western History Collections, University of Oklahoma Library (2); NAA, Smithsonian Institution, no. 45113-A. **138:** Map by Maryland CartoGraphics, Inc. **140:** National Museum of American Art, Washington, D.C./Art Resource, New York. **141:** Staatliche Museen zu Berlin-Preussischer Kulturbesitz, Museum für Völkerkunde, foto Dietrich Graf. **142:** © Richard Day. **143:** NAA, Smithsonian Institution, no. 44-261-E. **146, 147:** Western History Collections, University of Oklahoma Library (2); Archives and Manuscripts Division of the Oklahoma Historical Society. **148, 149:** Archives and Manuscripts Division of the Oklahoma Historical Society; © John Elk III; Western History Collections, University of Oklahoma Library. **150:** Courtesy Scripps Howard Broadcasting Company and Television Station KJRH, Tulsa, Oklahoma—NAA, Smithsonian Institution, no. 55, 301. **151:** Western History Collections, University of Oklahoma Library. **152, 153:** Courtesy Scripps Howard Broadcasting Company and Television Station KJRH, Tulsa, Oklahoma; copyright British Museum, London; courtesy Cherokee Heritage Center, Tahlequah, Oklahoma, photographed by Steve Tuttle—copyright British Museum, London—courtesy Scripps Howard Broadcasting Company and Television Station KJRH, Tulsa, Oklahoma. **154, 155:** Archives and Manuscripts Division of the Oklahoma Historical Society—courtesy Five Civilized Tribes Museum, Muskogee, Oklahoma, photographed by Steve Tuttle. **156, 157:** Courtesy Choctaw Community News, photographed by Julie Kelsey, except Choctaw princess photographed by Sharon Marritt. **159:** © Carole Thompson. **160:** Copyright British Museum, London; from *Indian Corn in Old America* by Paul Weatherwax, The MacMillan Company, New York, 1954. **161:** Painting by Ken Woodward, Springdale, Arkansas. **162, 163:** Staatliche Museen zu Berlin-Preussischer Kulturbesitz, Kunstbibliothek (2)—courtesy James Jerome Hill Reference Library, Saint Paul, Minnesota—courtesy The Chickasaw Nation, Ada, Oklahoma. **164:** Archives and Manuscripts Division of the Oklahoma Historical Society—courtesy Five Civilized Tribes Museum, Muskogee, Oklahoma, photographed by Steve Tuttle. **165:** Great Smoky Mountains National Park—copyright British Museum, London; Alabama Department of Archives and History, Montgomery, Alabama. **166:** Staatliche Museen zu Berlin-Preussischer Kulturbesitz, Kunstbibliothek—Archives and Manuscripts Division of the Oklahoma Historical Society—copyright British Museum, London. **167:** Stephanie B. Berryhill, courtesy Muscogee (Creek) Nation Communications Department, Okmulgee, Oklahoma. **168, 169:** Fil Hunter.

INDEX